OVERVIEW

# British Literature

## Curriculum Overview
## Elective

### OBJECTIVES

1. The student will gain a general overview of the development of British literature and thought from the Middle Ages to the Twentieth Century.

2. The student will learn to critique the philosophy of each author from a Christian perspective.

3. The student will become aware of the philosophies and religious beliefs that influenced the authors in each period of history.

4. The student will gain knowledge of the historical and biographical background of each author and period.

5. The student will appreciate literature as a reflection of the thought and life of the times.

| British Literature  LIFEPAC I | British Literature  LIFEPAC 2 |
|---|---|

**The Middle Ages**

INTRODUCTION AND
OLD ENGLISH LITERATURE

**A. Introduction**
**B. Old English Literature**

Bede–Ecclesiastical History of the
    English People

*Beowulf*

**Middle English Literature**

Chaucer

*Canterbury Tales–The Prologue,*
        *The Pardoner's Tale,*
        *Piers Plowman*

**Morality Plays and Prose Fiction**

*Everyman*

Sir Thomas Malory–*Le Morte d' Arthur*

---

**The Sixteenth Century**

**The Renaissance and Reformation**

INTRODUCTION AND
THE EARLY RENAISSANCE

Sir Thomas Moore

Roger Ascham

John Foxe

**Renaissance Poets**

Sir Thomas Wyatt the Elder

Sir Philip Sydney

Edmund Spenser

Mary (Sydney) Herbert,
    Countess of Pembroke

**Renaissance Prose and Drama**

Sir Walter Raleigh

William Shakespeare

The English Bible

| British Literature LIFEPAC 3 | British Literature LIFEPAC 4 |
|---|---|

**The Seventeenth and Eighteenth Centuries**

**The Stuarts and the Puritan Revolution (1603–1660)**

INTRODUCTION

John Donne

Ben Johnson

Francis Bacon

**More Seventeenth Century Writers**

John Milton

John Owen

Francis Bacon

**The Restoration and Neoclassical Period 1660–1785**

INTRODUCTION

John Dryden

John Bunyan

Jonathan Swift

Alexander Pope

Isaac Watts

**The Nineteenth Century (1798–1900)**

INTRODUCTION

**The Early Romantic Era**

William Blake

William Wordsworth

Samuel Taylor Coleridge

Sir Walter Scott

**The Late Romantic Era**

Jane Austen

Charles Lamb

George Gordon–Lord Byron

Percy Bysshe Shelley

John Keats

**The Victorian Era**

INTRODUCTION

Thomas Carlyle

John Henry Cardinal Newman

Lord Alfred Tennyson

Charles John Huffman Dickens

Robert Browning

George Eliot (Mary Ann Evans)

Oscar Wilde

Lewis Carroll (Charles Lutwidge Dodson)

## British Literature  LIFEPAC 5

### The Twentieth Century

INTRODUCTION

Thomas Hardy

Joseph Conrad

G. K. Chesterton

### Modern Poetry, Drama, and Prose

William Butler Yeats

T. S. Eliot

George Bernard Shaw

Winston Churchill

### Modern Fiction

Virginia Woolf

James Joyce

Aldous Leonard Huxley

C. S. Lewis

# MANAGEMENT

## STRUCTURE OF THE LIFEPAC CURRICULUM

The LIFEPAC curriculum is conveniently structured to provide one teacher handbook containing teacher support material with answer keys and ten student worktexts for each subject at grade levels two through twelve. The worktext format of the LIFEPACs allows the student to read the textual information and complete workbook activities all in the same booklet. The easy to follow LIFEPAC numbering system lists the grade as the first number(s) and the last two digits as the number of the series. For example, the Language Arts LIFEPAC at the 6th grade level, 5th book in the series would be LAN0605.

Each LIFEPAC is divided into 3 to 5 sections and begins with an introduction or overview of the booklet as well as a series of specific learning objectives to give a purpose to the study of the LIFEPAC. The introduction and objectives are followed by a vocabulary section which may be found at the beginning of each section at the lower levels, at the beginning of the LIFEPAC in the middle grades, or in the glossary at the high school level. Vocabulary words are used to develop word recognition and should not be confused with the spelling words introduced later in the LIFEPAC. The student should learn all vocabulary words before working the LIFEPAC sections to improve comprehension, retention, and reading skills.

Each activity or written assignment has a number for easy identification, such as 1.1. The first number corresponds to the LIFEPAC section and the number to the right of the decimal is the number of the activity.

Teacher checkpoints, which are essential to maintain quality learning, are found at various locations throughout the LIFEPAC. The teacher should check 1) neatness of work and penmanship, 2) quality of understanding (tested with a short oral quiz), 3) thoroughness of answers (complete sentences and paragraphs, correct spelling, etc.), 4) completion of activities (no blank spaces), and 5) accuracy of answers as compared to the answer key (all answers correct).

The self test questions are also number coded for easy reference. For example, 2.015 means that this is the 15th question in the self test of Section II. The first number corresponds to the LIFEPAC section, the zero indicates that it is a self test question, and the number to the right of the zero the question number.

The LIFEPAC test is packaged at the centerfold of each LIFEPAC. It should be removed and put aside before giving the booklet to the student for study.

Answer and test keys have the same numbering system as the LIFEPACs and appear at the back of this handbook. The student may be given access to the answer keys (not the test keys) under teacher supervision so that he can score his own work.

A thorough study of the Curriculum Overview by the teacher before instruction begins is essential to the success of the student. The teacher should become familiar with expected skill mastery and understand how these grade level skills fit into the overall skill development of the curriculum. The teacher should also preview the objectives that appear at the beginning of each LIFEPAC for additional preparation and planning.

### TEST SCORING and GRADING

Answer keys and test keys give examples of correct answers. They convey the idea, but the student may use many ways to express a correct answer. The teacher should check for the essence of the answer, not for the exact wording. Many questions are high level and require thinking and creativity on the part of the student. Each answer should be scored based on whether or not the main idea written by the student matches the model example. "Any Order" or "Either Order" in a key indicates that no particular order is necessary to be correct.

Most self tests and LIFEPAC tests at the lower elementary levels are scored at 1 point per question; however, the upper levels may have a point system awarding 2 to 5 points for various questions. Further, the total test points will vary; they may not always equal 100 points. They may be 78, 85, 100, 105, etc.

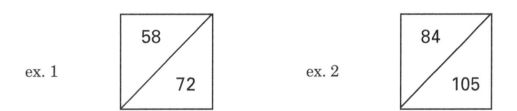

ex. 1     58 / 72       ex. 2     84 / 105

A score box similar to ex.1 above is located at the end of each self test and on the front of the LIFEPAC test. The bottom score, 72, represents the total number of points possible on the test. The upper score, 58, represents the number of points your student will need to receive an 80% or passing grade. If you wish to establish the exact percentage that your student has achieved, find the total points of his correct answers and divide it by the bottom number (in this case 72.) For example, if your student has a point total of 65, divide 65 by 72 for a grade of 90%. Referring to ex. 2, on a test with a total of 105 possible points, the student would have to receive a minimum of 84 correct points for an 80% or passing grade. If your student has received 93 points, simply divide the 93 by 105 for a percentage grade of 89%. Students who receive a score below 80% should review the LIFEPAC and retest using the appropriate Alternate Test found in the Teacher's Guide.

The following is a guideline to assign letter grades for completed LIFEPACs based on a maximum total score of 100 points.

LIFEPAC Test    =    60% of the Total Score (or percent grade)

Self Test    =    25% of the Total Score (average percent of self tests)

Reports    =    10% or 10* points per LIFEPAC

Oral Work    =    5% or 5* points per LIFEPAC

*Determined by the teacher's subjective evaluation of the student's daily work.

Example:

| | | | | | | |
|---|---|---|---|---|---|---|
| LIFEPAC Test Score | = | 92% | 92 x .60 | | = | 55 points |
| Self Test Average | = | 90% | 90 x .25 | | = | 23 points |
| Reports | | | | | = | 8 points |
| Oral Work | | | | | = | 4 points |

---

TOTAL POINTS                                    =    90 points


Grade Scale based on point system:    100  –  94  =  A

                                      93  –  86  =  B

                                      85  –  77  =  C

                                      76  –  70  =  D

                                Below      70  =  F

## *TEACHER HINTS and STUDYING TECHNIQUES*

LIFEPAC Activities are written to check the level of understanding of the preceding text. The student may look back to the text as necessary to complete these activities; however, a student should never attempt to do the activities without reading (studying) the text first. Self tests and LIFEPAC tests are never open book tests.

Language arts activities (skill integration) often appear within other subject curriculum. The purpose is to give the student an opportunity to test his skill mastery outside of the context in which it was presented.

Writing complete answers (paragraphs) to some questions is an integral part of the LIFEPAC Curriculum in all subjects. This builds communication and organization skills, increases understanding and retention of ideas, and helps enforce good penmanship. Complete sentences should be encouraged for this type of activity. Obviously, single words or phrases do not meet the intent of the activity, since multiple lines are given for the response.

Review is essential to student success. Time invested in review where review is suggested will be time saved in correcting errors later. Self tests, unlike the section activities, are closed book. This procedure helps to identify weaknesses before they become too great to overcome. Certain objectives from self tests are cumulative and test previous sections; therefore, good preparation for a self test must include all material studied up to that testing point.

The following procedure checklist has been found to be successful in developing good study habits in the LIFEPAC curriculum.

1. Read the introduction and Table of Contents.
2. Read the objectives.
3. Recite and study the entire vocabulary (glossary) list.
4. Study each section as follows:
    a. Read the introduction and study the section objectives.
    b. Read all the text for the entire section, but answer none of the activities.
    c. Return to the beginning of the section and memorize each vocabulary word and definition.
    d. Reread the section, complete the activities, check the answers with the answer key, correct all errors, and have the teacher check.
    e. Read the self test but do not answer the questions.
    f. Go to the beginning of the first section and reread the text and answers to the activities up to the self test you have not yet done.
    g. Answer the questions to the self test without looking back.
    h. Have the self test checked by the teacher.
    i. Correct the self test and have the teacher check the corrections.
    j. Repeat steps a–i for each section.

5. Use the SQ3R* method to prepare for the LIFEPAC test.
6. Take the LIFEPAC test as a closed book test.
7. LIFEPAC tests are administered and scored under direct teacher supervision. Students who receive scores below 80% should review the LIFEPAC using the SQ3R* study method and take the Alternate Test located in the Teacher Handbook. The final test grade may be the grade on the Alternate Test or an average of the grades from the original LIFEPAC test and the Alternate Test.

    *SQ3R:  **S**can the whole LIFEPAC.

    **Q**uestion yourself on the objectives.

    **R**ead the whole LIFEPAC again.

    **R**ecite through an oral examination.

    **R**eview weak areas.

## GOAL SETTING and SCHEDULES

Each school must develop its own schedule, because no single set of procedures will fit every situation. The following is an example of a daily schedule that includes the five LIFEPAC subjects as well as time slotted for special activities.

Possible Daily Schedule

| | | | |
|---|---|---|---|
| 8:15 | – | 8:25 | Pledges, prayer, songs, devotions, etc. |
| 8:25 | – | 9:10 | Bible |
| 9:10 | – | 9:55 | Language Arts |
| | | | |
| 9:55 | – | 10:15 | Recess (juice break) |
| | | | |
| 10:15 | – | 11:00 | Mathematics |
| 11:00 | – | 11:45 | History & Geography |
| | | | |
| 11:45 | – | 12:30 | Lunch, recess, quiet time |
| | | | |
| 12:30 | – | 1:15 | Science |
| 1:15 | – | | Drill, remedial work, enrichment* |

*Enrichment: Computer time, physical education, field trips, fun reading, games and puzzles, family business, hobbies, resource persons, guests, crafts, creative work, electives, music appreciation, projects.

Basically, two factors need to be considered when assigning work to a student in the LIFEPAC curriculum.

The first is time. An average of 45 minutes should be devoted to each subject, each day. Remember, this is only an average. Because of extenuating circumstances a student may spend only 15 minutes on a subject one day and the next day spend 90 minutes on the same subject.

The second factor is the number of pages to be worked in each subject. A single LIFEPAC is designed to take 3 to 4 weeks to complete. Allowing about 3-4 days for LIFEPAC introduction, review, and tests, the student has approximately 15 days to complete the LIFEPAC pages. Simply take the number of pages in the LIFEPAC, divide it by 15 and you will have the number of pages that must be completed on a daily basis to keep the student on schedule. For example, a LIFEPAC containing 45 pages will require 3 completed pages per day. Again, this is only an average. While working a 45 page LIFEPAC, the student may complete only 1 page the first day if the text has a lot of activities or reports, but go on to complete 5 pages the next day.

Long range planning requires some organization. Because the traditional school year originates in the early fall of one year and continues to late spring of the following year, a calendar should be devised that covers this period of time. Approximate beginning and completion dates can be noted on the calendar as well as special occasions such as holidays, vacations and birthdays. Since each LIFEPAC takes 3-4 weeks or eighteen days to complete, it should take about 180 school days to finish a set of ten LIFEPACs. Starting at the beginning school date, mark off eighteen school days on the calendar and that will become the targeted completion date for the first LIFEPAC. Continue marking the calendar until you have established dates for the remaining nine LIFEPACs making adjustments for previously noted holidays and vacations. If all five subjects are being used, the ten established target dates should be the same for the LIFEPACs in each subject.

## *FORMS*

The sample weekly lesson plan and student grading sheet forms are included in this section as teacher support materials and may be duplicated at the convenience of the teacher.

The student grading sheet is provided for those who desire to follow the suggested guidelines for assignment of letter grades found on page 3 of this section. The student's self test scores should be posted as percentage grades. When the LIFEPAC is completed the teacher should average the self test grades, multiply the average by .25 and post the points in the box marked self test points. The LIFEPAC percentage grade should be multiplied by .60 and posted. Next, the teacher should award and post points for written reports and oral work. A report may be any type of written work assigned to the student whether it is a LIFEPAC or additional learning activity. Oral work includes the student's ability to respond orally to questions which may or may not be related to LIFEPAC activities or any type of oral report assigned by the teacher. The points may then be totaled and a final grade entered along with the date that the LIFEPAC was completed.

The Student Record Book which was specifically designed for use with the Alpha Omega curriculum provides space to record weekly progress for one student over a nine week period as well as a place to post self test and LIFEPAC scores. The Student Record Books are available through the current Alpha Omega catalog; however, unlike the enclosed forms these books are not for duplication and should be purchased in sets of four to cover a full academic year.

| WEEKLY LESSON PLANNER | | | |
|---|---|---|---|
| | | | **Week of:** |
| Subject | Subject | Subject | Subject |
| **Monday** | | | |
| Subject | Subject | Subject | Subject |
| **Tuesday** | | | |
| Subject | Subject | Subject | Subject |
| **Wednesday** | | | |
| Subject | Subject | Subject | Subject |
| | | | |
| Subject | Subject | Subject | Subject |
| | | | |

19

# WEEKLY LESSON PLANNER

**Week of:**

| Subject | Subject | Subject | Subject |
|---------|---------|---------|---------|
| **Monday** | | | |

| Subject | Subject | Subject | Subject |
|---------|---------|---------|---------|
| **Tuesday** | | | |

| Subject | Subject | Subject | Subject |
|---------|---------|---------|---------|
| **Wednesday** | | | |

| Subject | Subject | Subject | Subject |
|---------|---------|---------|---------|
| **Thursday** | | | |

| Subject | Subject | Subject | Subject |
|---------|---------|---------|---------|
| **Friday** | | | |

## Bible

| LP # | Self Test Scores by Sections 1 | 2 | 3 | 4 | 5 | Self Test Points | LIFEPAC Test | Oral Points | Report Points | Final Grade | Date |
|------|---|---|---|---|---|---|---|---|---|---|---|
| 01 | | | | | | | | | | | |
| 02 | | | | | | | | | | | |
| 03 | | | | | | | | | | | |
| 04 | | | | | | | | | | | |
| 05 | | | | | | | | | | | |
| 06 | | | | | | | | | | | |
| 07 | | | | | | | | | | | |
| 08 | | | | | | | | | | | |
| 09 | | | | | | | | | | | |
| 10 | | | | | | | | | | | |

## History & Geography

| LP # | Self Test Scores by Sections 1 | 2 | 3 | 4 | 5 | Self Test Points | LIFEPAC Test | Oral Points | Report Points | Final Grade | Date |
|------|---|---|---|---|---|---|---|---|---|---|---|
| 01 | | | | | | | | | | | |
| 02 | | | | | | | | | | | |
| 03 | | | | | | | | | | | |
| 04 | | | | | | | | | | | |
| 05 | | | | | | | | | | | |
| 06 | | | | | | | | | | | |
| 07 | | | | | | | | | | | |
| 08 | | | | | | | | | | | |
| 09 | | | | | | | | | | | |
| 10 | | | | | | | | | | | |

## Language Arts

| LP # | Self Test Scores by Sections 1 | 2 | 3 | 4 | 5 | Self Test Points | LIFEPAC Test | Oral Points | Report Points | Final Grade | Date |
|------|---|---|---|---|---|---|---|---|---|---|---|
| 01 | | | | | | | | | | | |
| 02 | | | | | | | | | | | |
| 03 | | | | | | | | | | | |
| 04 | | | | | | | | | | | |
| 05 | | | | | | | | | | | |
| 06 | | | | | | | | | | | |
| 07 | | | | | | | | | | | |
| 08 | | | | | | | | | | | |
| 09 | | | | | | | | | | | |
| 10 | | | | | | | | | | | |

Student Name _____     Year _____

## Mathematics

| LP # | Self Test Scores by Sections 1 | 2 | 3 | 4 | 5 | Self Test Points | LIFEPAC Test | Oral Points | Report Points | Final Grade | Date |
|------|---|---|---|---|---|---|---|---|---|---|---|
| 01 | | | | | | | | | | | |
| 02 | | | | | | | | | | | |
| 03 | | | | | | | | | | | |
| 04 | | | | | | | | | | | |
| 05 | | | | | | | | | | | |
| 06 | | | | | | | | | | | |
| 07 | | | | | | | | | | | |
| 08 | | | | | | | | | | | |
| 09 | | | | | | | | | | | |
| 10 | | | | | | | | | | | |

## Science

| LP # | Self Test Scores by Sections 1 | 2 | 3 | 4 | 5 | Self Test Points | LIFEPAC Test | Oral Points | Report Points | Final Grade | Date |
|------|---|---|---|---|---|---|---|---|---|---|---|
| 01 | | | | | | | | | | | |
| 02 | | | | | | | | | | | |
| 03 | | | | | | | | | | | |
| 04 | | | | | | | | | | | |
| 05 | | | | | | | | | | | |
| 06 | | | | | | | | | | | |
| 07 | | | | | | | | | | | |
| 08 | | | | | | | | | | | |
| 09 | | | | | | | | | | | |
| 10 | | | | | | | | | | | |

## Spelling/Electives

| LP # | Self Test Scores by Sections 1 | 2 | 3 | 4 | 5 | Self Test Points | LIFEPAC Test | Oral Points | Report Points | Final Grade | Da |
|------|---|---|---|---|---|---|---|---|---|---|---|
| 01 | | | | | | | | | | | |
| 02 | | | | | | | | | | | |
| 03 | | | | | | | | | | | |
| 04 | | | | | | | | | | | |
| 05 | | | | | | | | | | | |
| 06 | | | | | | | | | | | |
| 07 | | | | | | | | | | | |
| 08 | | | | | | | | | | | |
| 09 | | | | | | | | | | | |
| 10 | | | | | | | | | | | |

NOTES

## INSTRUCTION FOR BRITISH LITERATURE

This course is one in a two-part literature series for high school students. The series complements AOP's current Language Arts program, adding a richness that can only be found in the great books of Western Civilization. The series is designed to enlarge the Christian's understanding of the development of Western Civilization while strengthening him or her in the faith. Its content and methodology utilize the principles of classical education. If applied properly, the inquisitive high school student can benefit greatly from a thorough analysis of the literature that has shaped Western Civilization.

The exercises presented in this course follow a path similar to the classical learning structure: grammar, logic, and rhetoric. Grammar is the basic facts or principles of a subject. Logic (or dialectic) is an understanding of how the facts relate to one another. Rhetoric is the ability to articulate and apply knowledge and understanding with eloquence and wisdom. A parallel structure can be found in Scripture: knowledge (Proverbs 1:7), understanding (Job 28:28), and wisdom (Eccl. 12:9).

The student is required to master the "grammar" of the course by completing short answer questions dispersed throughout the text. His knowledge of the course's "grammar" will be checked on Self Tests and Tests.

A logical understanding of the facts are encouraged through the "What to Look For" and "For Thought and Discussion" exercises. "What to Look For" exercises are included before certain readings. This encourages attentive reading and will prepare the student for the corresponding "For Thought and Discussion" exercises. "For Thought and Discussion" exercises are included at the end of each Self Test. They are meant to facilitate discussion between the student and the teacher on a specific subject for the means of developing a more thoroughly Christian worldview. A Scriptural understanding of the world is the goal of each "For Thought and Discussion" exercise. Discussion tips and subject helps for the teacher are available in the teacher notes. But, it is most helpful for the teacher to be intimately familiar with the subject matter. Reading along with the student is recommended.

Lastly, the goal of learning—wisdom—is encouraged through application and communication. This is done in the "Writing and Thinking" exercises at the end of each Test. In the "Writing and Thinking" exercises the student is asked to communicate in a clear and precise manner their application of select "For Thought and Discussion" exercises. This exercise will not be difficult IF the teacher has been diligent enough to guide the student through the "For Thought and Discussion" exercises.

With this method of learning, both teacher and student must be persistent. The exercises take work. But in the end, the student will reap a bounty of knowledge, understanding and wisdom to the glory of God.

**Selected Bibliography**

Listed below are writings that have been used and consulted in the creation of this work.
It is not a complete listing of the sources consulted.

Clive Staples Lewis, *The Discarded Image: An Introduction to Medieval and Renaissance Literature*
(Cambridge: Cambridge University Press, 1995).

Clive Staples Lewis, *Studies in Medieval and Renaissance Literature*
(Cambridge: Cambridge University Press, 1998).

Gene Edward Veith, *Reading Between the Lines: A Christian's Guide to Literature*
(Wheaton, IL: Crossway Books, 1990).

*Invitation to the Classics*, ed. Louise Cowan and Os Guinness (Grand Rapids, MI: Baker Books, 1998).

J. H. Merle d' Aubigné, *The Reformation in England*, vol. 1 & 2 (London: Banner of Truth Trust, 1963).

Otto Scott, *The Great Christian Revolution: How Christianity Transformed the World*
(Windsor, NY: The Reformer, 1995).

Peter Ackroyd, *Introduction to Dickens* (New York: Ballantine Books, 1992).

Peter J. Leithart, *Brightest Heaven of Invention: A Christian Guide to Six Shakespeare Plays*
(Moscow, ID: Canon Press, 1996).

*The Norton Anthology of British Literature*, vol. 1 & 2, ed. M. H. Abrams
(New York: W.W. Norton & Company, 1986).

*The Literature of Renaissance England, ed. John Hollander and Frank Kermode*
*(New York: Oxford University Press, 1973).*

*William Harmon and C. Hugh Holman, Handbook to Literature*
*(Upper Saddle River, NJ: Prentice Hall, 1996).*

**British Literature-Related Web Sites**
If any of the Web Site addresses do not work, enter the name in a search engine.

Anthology of English Literature: Middle English to Seventeenth Century
http://www.luminarium.org/medlit/

Eighteenth Century Resources http://andromeda.rutgers.edu/~jlynch/18th/

Old English Pages at Georgetown University http://www.georgetown.edu/cball/oe/old_english.html

Spartacus Internet Encyclopedia: British History 1700-1950
http://www.spartacus.schoolnet.co.uk/industry.html

The Victorian Web http://landow.stg.brown.edu/victorian/victov.html

"Voice of the Shuttle ucsb" Web Pages for Humanities Research: English Literature
http://vos.ucsb.edu/shuttle/english.html

Project Gutenberg Index http://www.mirrors.org.sg/pg/

T
E
S
T
S

**Reproducible Tests**
for use with the American Literature
Teacher's Guide

## BRITISH LITERATURE LIFEPAC ONE ALTERNATE TEST

**Name** _____

**Date** _____

**Score** _____

80 / 100

**Underline the correct answer in each of the following statements** (each answer, 2 points).

1. Caedmon's Hymn is the first record of religious poem written in (Italian, French, Old English).

2. In 1382, (John Wycliffe, St. Thomas Aquinas, Pope Gregory) translated the Holy Scriptures into the language of the common man.

3. Chaucer was a careful observer of (human, animal, mother) nature.

4. Much of Chaucer's work is based on literary models from classical, (Polish, Italian, Scandinavian) and French literature.

5. *The Canterbury Tales* is a/an (finished, unfinished) collection of tales.

6. Prior to the Reformation, the church used (picture boards, overheads, plays) instead of the preaching of Scripture to educate the illiterate.

7. *The Ecclesiastical History of the English People* is a revelation of the unfolding providence of God in (Italy, Paris, England).

8. Chaucer was born and raised as a member of the (aristocracy, poor, middle) class.

9. *Everyman* is the most famous (morality, mystery) play of the Middle Ages.

10. (Mystery, Morality) plays were often performed as part of a series.

11. (Mysteries, Moralities) dramatized the moral struggle of the common man by allegorizing vices and virtues.

12. The theological basis of *Everyman* is (Evangelical, Mormon, Roman Catholic).

**Answer** *true* **or** *false* **for each of the following statements** (each answer, 2 points).

13. _____ The name of the monster in Beowulf is Grendel.

14. _____ Beowulf is most eager that God receive praise.

15. _____ Caedmon learned about the origin of man, the departure of Israel out of Egypt, and the preaching of the Apostles from personal study of the Scriptures.

16. _____ Bede said that it was impossible to make a literal translation of a poem without loosing some of its beauty and dignity.

17. _____ The pilgrims were headed to Canterbury to seek the "holy blessed martyr," Sir Thomas Becket.

18. _____ The Knight is truly a gentleman, who loved chivalry, truth, honor, freedom and all courtesy.

19. _____ The Wife of Bath wore scarlet red stockings, had been married five times and had been on pilgrimages to Jerusalem and Rome.

20. _____ The pilgrim that told the best tale would win a dinner at the expense of the other pilgrims.

21. _____ The Pardoner's theme is "the love of money is the root of all evil."

22. _____ The Pardoner stops his tale to preach on the good of drinking, gambling, swearing and gluttony.

23. _____ In the Pardoner's tale, the three young men find a treasure of gold underneath a tree.

24. _____ Knowledge advises Everyman not to go to Priesthood to receive the holy sacrament, extreme unction.

25. _____ In *Piers Plowman*, the Friars were explaining Scripture in a way that would benefit themselves.

26. _____ The parish priests and the pardoners, in Piers' vision, gave all that they had to the poor.

27. _____ Beauty, Discretion, Strength and the Five-Wits depart from Everyman when they discover that he is headed for the grave.

28. _____ Knowledge descends into the grave with Everyman.

29. _____ According to lines 905–909 of *Everyman*, the good deeds of Christ will bring us help before God.

30. _____ Sir Gawain exposes Lancelot and Guenevere to the knights and suggests that the king be told of their adulterous love.

31. _____ Sir Gawain rescues Guenevere and slays everyone that stood against them.

32. _____ King Arthur is mortally wounded as he slays Sir Lucan.

33. _____ King Arthur commands Bedivere three times to throw Excalibur into the lake.

34. _____ A sea monster catches the sword and swallows it.

35. _____ Everyone is certain that King Arthur is dead.

36. _____ After the death of Guenevere, Sir Lancelot soon dies.

**Fill in each of the blanks using items from the word list below** (each answer, 2 points).

| | | |
|---|---|---|
| heroic | *Beowulf* | King Arthur |
| church | Yorkist | neighbor |
| French | worldview | Anglo-Saxons |
| Scotland | *Le Morte d' Arthur* | Middle |
| Rome | Norman | |

37. The Middle Ages began with the fall of _____ in 476 and ended with the Renaissance in Italy in 1300.

38. Old English developed out of the language that was spoken by the Germanic invaders known as the _____ .

39. Middle English developed some time after the _____ conquest.

40. The romance began to take shape during the _____ English period.

41. The character Beowulf embodies the _____ ideal.

42. The author of *Piers Plowman* wrote satirically of the _____ and its corruption, and called for its reform.

43.　The central theme of Piers Plowman is love for God and love for _____ .

44.　He was imprisoned in 1468 for his involvement in the Lancastrian revolt against the _____ king, Edward IV.

45.　While in prison, Malory began and completed _____ .

46.　*Le Morte d' Arthur* is a compilation of all the people and places that had been associated with the story of _____ and his knights.

47.　The poet of *Beowulf* attempted to combine the heroic ideal and Christian doctrine under one _____ .

48.　_____ is an example of a heroic narrative that ensured a king enduring fame.

49.　William and his descendants encouraged the influence of _____ culture on the English people.

50.　Columba was an Irish missionary devoted to the preaching of the Gospel in _____ .

# BRITISH LITERATURE LIFEPAC TWO ALTERNATE TEST

**Name** _____

**Date** _____

**Score** _____

91 / 114

**Underline the correct answer in each of the following statements** (each answer, 2 points).

1. The Protestant Reformers in England believed that (the church, Scripture, the king) alone was the guide to faith and life.

2. The (Renaissance, Reformation, Middle Ages) was a human-centered movement.

3. The ideals of the Renaissance and the Reformation shaped (Elizabethan, Classical, Modern) literature.

4. During his time, Sir Philip Sidney was considered the near perfect (writer, courtier, soldier).

5. Sidney completed the first (epic, play, sonnet sequence) in England known as *Astrophil and Stella*.

6. A (tragedy, comedy) seeks primarily to (frighten, amuse, horrify).

7. The (pastoral, sonnet, short story) was the chief literary device imported from Italy.

8. (Sir Thomas More, Roger Ascham, William Tyndale) used Erasmus' Greek New Testament to translate the Bible into English.

9. During the reign of (Edward VI, Mary, Elizabeth), nearly 300 (Protestants, Catholics, Jews) were burned at the stake for their faith.

10. In her rendering of Psalm 58, the Countess of Pembroke compares the (wicked, righteous, godly) to snakes.

11. Sir Walter Raleigh was a soldier and a seaman as well as a philosopher, a historian and a (prince, merchant, poet).

12. During Elizabethan times, the public theaters were (square, rectangle, oval) shaped with several tiers of seating.

13. William Shakespeare was born in (Stratford-on-Avon, London, Edinburgh).

14. The tragedies, *Hamlet*, *Macbeth*, *King Lear* and *Othello*, dramatize the (fall, success, triumph) of man.

15. The Complete Edition of Shakespeare's Works, also known as the (First Folio, First Quarto, First Book), was first published in (1599, 1603, 1623).

16. The English (Renaissance, Enlightenment, Reformation) was a revolution of heart and mind based on the teachings of a single book, the Bible.

17. First published in 1560, The (Geneva Bible, Great Bible, Latin Vulgate) was the first translation to include marginal notes and divide the passages by numbered verses.

18. The editors of the (King James Version, Geneva Bible, Great Bible) avoided the most literal or direct translation, inserting words or phrases that would be most clearly understood by the (scholars, priests, people).

**Answer** *true* **or** *false* **for each of the following statements** (each answer, 2 points).

19. _____ The Utopians, of Sir Thomas More's book, value gold and silver highly.

20. _____ Before being burned at the stake, Thomas Cranmer denounced his recantation and called the pope Christ's enemy.

21. _____ In *The Schoolmaster*, Roger Ascham recommends punishment as the best thing to "sharpen a good wit" and "encourage a will to learning."

22. _____ According to Ascham, the fastest way to entangle the mind with false doctrine is first to entice the will to immoral living.

23. _____ Before he was burned at the stake, Hugh Latimer turned to Nicholas Ridley and said, "Be of good cheer, Ridley; and play the man. We shall this day, by God's grace, light up such a candle in England, as I trust, will never be put out."

24. _____ The "murdering boy" in Sonnet 20 of Sidney's sonnet sequence *Astrophil and Stella* is Cupid.

25. _____ In *Defense of Posey*, Sidney asserts that the purpose of writing fiction and poetry is to teach and delight.

26. _____ In *The Faerie Queen*, the lovely lady is representative of truth and true religion.

27. _____ The lovely lady instructs the knight to add faith to his force so that he might be able to escape the power of Error.

28. _____ According to the last stanza of Sir Walter Raleigh's "The Nymph's answer to the Shepherd," if the joys of romance never ended then the speaker might be moved to be the shepherd's love.

29. _____ In his *History of the World,* Raleigh comments that man has divine understanding so that he may serve himself.

30. _____ Raleigh stated in his *History of the World* that the animals have the intellect of angels and the sensual nature of man.

31. _____ *The Taming of the Shrew* is a tragedy that is a play-within-a-play.

32. _____ In *The Taming of the Shrew*, Christopher Sly is dressed up in his Lord's clothes and told that he has been insane for many years.

33. _____ Baptista will not allow Katherine to be courted until Bianca is married.

34. _____ Katherine and Petruchio fight over the meanings of various words.

35. _____ Petruchio says that taming Kate is like training a falcon.

36. _____ At the end of the play, Kate tells the other women that a husband is the "head" of the wife and the "one that cares for" her.

**Fill in each of the blanks using items from the word list below** (each answer, 2 points).

| | | |
|---|---|---|
| Geneva | *Utopia* | historical |
| conceit | three | divine |
| fourteen | Sir Philip Sidney | English |
| archaic | learning | England |
| Scripture | rare | ever-fixed |
| octave | | |

33

37. John Foxe wrote *Acts and Monuments* as a _____ testament to the fact that Evangelicalism has been persecuted throughout the centuries because it embodies the true Biblical faith.

38. Sir Thomas More's masterpiece, _____ , is a fantastical vision of a New World free of societal ills.

39. Roger Ascham believed that the study of certain Latin and Greek classics in subjection to the authority of _____ was a means to "truth in religion, honesty of living, and right order in _____ ."

40. Sir Thomas Wyatt introduced the Italian sonnet into _____ .

41. A _____ is an elaborate comparison made by the poet within the sonnet.

42. *The Faerie Queen* is an epic that uses _____ language and medieval symbols of _____ .

43. The Countess of Pembroke was known as " _____ poet."

44. The Countess edited and completed works by her brother, _____ .

45. According to line 5 of Shakespeare's Sonnet 116, true love is an " _____ mark."

46. Despite her "imperfections," the poet of Sonnet 116 thinks that his mistress is " _____ ."

47. In the selected readings from Isaiah, the last sentence of the King James text matches the last two sentences of the _____ Bible.

48. The _____ rhyme scheme became the most popular sonnet form of the Elizabethan period.

49. Henry Howard, the earl of Surrey, structured the sonnet into _____ quatrains and a couplet: abab cdcd efef gg.

50. The Italian sonnet contains _____ lines, which are arranged into a/an _____ and a sestet.

## BRITISH LITERATURE LIFEPAC THREE ALTERNATE TEST

**Name** _____

**Date** _____

**Score** _____

82 / 103

**Answer** *true* **or** *false* **for each of the following statements** (each answer, 2 points).

1. _____ Much of the literature written during the seventeenth century was indifferent to morals and government.

2. _____ The Metaphysical poets rejected the conventions of Elizabethan poetry and wrote complex, allusive and obscure poems.

3. _____ The divine right of kings established the people's will as sovereign.

4. _____ Charles I was executed because he plotted to overthrow the "Rights and liberties of the People."

5. _____ Middle-class people that believed a man's conscience should be self-governed supported Parliamentary forces during the Puritan Revolution.

6. _____ According to Bacon's essay, "Of Truth," the sovereign good of human nature is the pursuit of pleasure.

7. _____ Charles II was welcomed back to England as the great deliverer.

8. _____ The Whig party favored the supremacy of the monarchy and the Anglican Church.

9. _____ The Glorious Revolution ushered in a time of religious and political toleration.

10. _____ Advances in science and philosophy helped to erode superstitious beliefs about the natural world.

11. _____ The Age of Reason exalted man's intellectual and moral abilities.

12. _____ Many of the writers during the Neoclassical period wrote in a simple, clear, and polished style.

13. _____ According to the hymn "Alas, and Did My Savior Bleed?," the poet is overwhelmed with feelings of doubt.

14. _____ According to the hymn "How Shall the Young Secure Their Hearts," the physical universe gives us a more complete knowledge of God and His requirements of us.

**Underline the correct answer in each of the following statements** (each answer, 3 points).

15. As a (Royalist, Parliamentary supporter, Cavalier), Milton wrote pamphlets on education, freedom of the press, and the reformation of the church.

16. Dryden's innovative work within classical genres set the boundaries of (Romantic, Renaissance, Neoclassical) literature.

17. In his satirical works, particularly *Gulliver's Travels*, Swift sought to cast derision on the (Christian, Renaissance, Enlightenment) concept of human perfectibility.

18. As a clergyman in the Anglican Church and advocate of royal supremacy, Swift served as editor for the (Tory, Whig) party paper, the *Examiner*.

19. Isaac Watts composed over 600 (hymns, essays, novels) and is known as the Father of English (poetry, criticism, hymnody).

20. Watts' poetry is written in the concise, simple style of the (Romantic, Neoclassical, Renaissance) period.

21. George Herbert used (poetry, novels, essays) as a means to renewed spiritual fervor.

22. In the epic (*Areopagitica, Lycidas, Paradise Lost*), Milton attempts to "justify the ways of God to men."

**Fill in each of the blanks using items from the following word list** (each answer, 2 points).

| | | |
|---|---|---|
| Greek | Roman | Oliver Cromwell |
| Cavalier | preaching | Bible |
| physical | metaphysical | man |
| | allegories | |

23. The _____ poets sought to emulate Ben Jonson's classical styled poetry.

24. Francis Bacon's writings on "knowledge" helped revolutionize mankind's approach to the _____ world.

25. John Owen became one of four main preachers to the Rump Parliament, and served as an advisor to _____ in ecclesiastical matters.

26. John Donne's " _____ wit" can be seen in his love poetry as well as in his religious works.

27. John Bunyan wrote one of the greatest _____ in English literature.

28. Bunyan was imprisoned several times for _____ .

29. The parables used in *Pilgrim's Progress* are similar to those found in the _____ .

30. Alexander Pope modeled himself after the ancient _____ and _____ poets.

31. As a rationalist, Pope asserted that _____ was the "sole judge of truth."

**Circle the letter of the lines that best answers the following questions** (each answer, 2 points).

32. According to *Pilgrim's Progress*, when does Christian first come under conviction for his sin?

    a. after reading in his book that he is condemned to die

    b. after he falls into the Slough of Despond

    c. after he decides to travel to the Celestial City

    d. after he talks to Mr. Worldly-Wiseman

33. When did Christian's burden fall from his back?

    a. when Christian visited Mr. Legality

    b. when Christian came up to the cross

    c. when Christian pulled himself out of the Slough of Despond

    d. when Christian visited Vanity Fair

34. Why is the town Vanity Fair named so?

    a. all that is in the town is full of spiritual significance

    b. the town has a few Christians living in it

    c. the town is full of beautiful people

    d. all that is in the town is vanity or worthless

35. According to Dryden's poem "Astrea Redux," why does the poet compare Charles II to King David?

    a. David sinned grievously.

    b. David was chosen by God to rule Israel.

    c. David committed adultery.

    d. The nation of Israel elected David into office.

36. How does the poet describe the nation's changed attitude toward their actions during the Puritan Revolution?

    a. joyous

    b. confused

    c. repentant

    d. bewildered

37. According to *Gulliver's Travels*, how does Swift satirize and trivialize the significant conflict between Protestants and Catholics?

    a. He characterizes their differences as nothing more than differing opinions on which end to break open an egg.

    b. He characterizes their differences as if they were two spotted pigs fighting.

    c. He describes the Catholics as a spotted panther.

    d. He characterizes their differences as nothing more than the height of the heel of their shoes.

38. What is ridiculous about the Lilliputians practice of rewarding people for obeying the law rather than punishing them for disobeying it?

    a. It assumes that people will not want to obey the law

    b. It assumes that people are good at heart

    c. It assumes that punishment is the best incentive

    d. It assumes that people are sinful

39. According to Alexander Pope's "An Essay on Man," what is the limitations of man's knowledge?

    a. Scripture

    b. supernatural occurrences

    c. nature

    d. God's law

40. To what purpose did George Herbert shape his poem, "Easter Wings," into the form of wings?

    a. to make a pretty picture

    b. to reinforce the message of the poem

    c. to make the message more complex

    d. he had no purpose

41.     The story of *Paradise Lost* centers around what?

    a.  Satan's fall from heaven

    b.  Adam and Eve's freedom to choose good or evil

    c.  God's election of His chosen people

    d.  Mankind's inability to choose good or evil

42.     In his sermon, "Righteous Zeal Encouraged by Divine Protection," what does John Owen call "treacherous contrivances against the God of heaven?"

    a.  the justification of and compliance with wicked actions

    b.  the punishment of wicked actions

    c.  the negligent administration of authority

    d.  the pursuit of God's glory in civil affairs

43.     In his "An Essay of Man," Pope attempts to do what?

    a.  give an apology for the sinfulness of man

    b.  explain why man sinned against God in the garden

    c.  "vindicate the ways of God to man"

    d.  "justify the ways of God to man"

44.     In Donne's poem "A Valediction: Forbidding Mourning," the poet compares himself and his beloved to what?

    a.  the branches of a tree bent by the wind

    b.  the feet of a compass

    c.  the sails of a ship

    d.  two stars in the sky

45.     Why does Jonson proclaim in his poem in memory of Shakespeare that Shakespeare is a poet "not of an age, but for all time?"

    a.  his works were not offensive to anyone

    b.  he tried to write like a metaphysical poet

    c.  the appeal and greatness of his work surpasses the boundaries of time and culture

    d.  he did not write for the common man

## BRITISH LITERATURE LIFEPAC FOUR ALTERNATE TEST

**Name** _____

**Date** _____

**Score** _____

82 / 103

**Answer** *true* **or** *false* **for each of the following statements** (each answer, 1 point).

1. _____ After the Napoleonic wars, England experienced an economic boom.

2. _____ The main target of Jane Austen's satire was the religious controversies of the day.

3. _____ In Shelley's "Ode to the West Wind," the West Wind is called the "Destroyer and preserver" because it destroys that which is dead and preserves new life.

4. _____ In *Don Juan*, Byron says that it is a pity that pleasure is a sin and sin is pleasurable.

5. _____ England experienced dynamic changes in the realms of politics, economics and religion during the Victorian era.

6. _____ Charles Darwin's theory of evolution caused many to doubt all traditional beliefs about mankind and society.

7. _____ Evangelicals were influential in the abolition of slavery and the enactment of child labor laws.

8. _____ The Oxford Movement emphasized the rituals and traditions of the Church of England.

9. _____ The Art for Art's Sake theorists believed that experience was the source of meaning.

10. _____ *Apologia pro Vita Sua* is the autobiographical account of Newman's spiritual quest for certainty, which he eventually found in the traditions and rituals of the Church of England.

11. _____ The Romantic Period of literature in England was inaugurated by the publication of *Songs of Experience* in 1798.

12. _____ In Wilde's play, *The Importance of Being Earnest*, it is important to Gwendolen that the man she marry is named "Earnest" because the sound of the name produces just the right vibrations.

13. _____ In *Alice in Wonderland*, Alice becomes frustrated with the game of croquet because nobody will let her bend the rules to win.

14. _____ In *Alice in Wonderland*, the Queen deals with any difficulty that she comes up against by crying.

15. _____ Coleridge's literary criticism reversed the traditional emphasis of poetry by focusing on poetry's ability to teach wisdom.

16. _____ The literature of the Romantic period in England is characterized by individualism, mysticism, emotionalism, love of nature, nostalgia, and a fascination with the medieval past.

17. _____ The opening line of *Pride and Prejudice* is ironic because in the story a single man in possession of a good fortune is *never* lacking of available women willing to become his wife.

**Underline the correct answer in each of the following statements** (each answer, 3 points).

18. In 1833 Thomas Carlyle published a philosophical satire outlining his spiritual idealism. It was entitled (*The French Revolution, On Heroes, Hero-Worship, Sartor Resartus*).

19. Carlyle's histories contend that the basis for strong, stable societies is (strong leaders, intelligent voters, God-fearing people).

20. In 1857 at the encouragement of Lewes, George Eliot published (*Middlemarch, Silas Marner, Scenes from Clerical Life*) in *Blackwood's Magazine*.

21. Eliot's belief in moral progress was influenced by the theory of (Higher Criticism, Evolution, Utilitarianism, Evangelicalism).

22. As a boy, Charles Dickens was made to work in a (factory, mine, lawyer's office) when his father was imprisoned for (stealing, unpaid debts, murder).

23. Published in volume form in 1837, (*The Pickwick Papers, Sketches by Boz, David Copperfield*) was the first book to make Dickens a celebrity in England and America.

24. In 1867–1868, Dickens traveled for the second time to America to give (public readings of his works, speeches on slavery, free lectures on social issues).

25. Written by Tennyson for his friend Hallam, (*Poems, In Memoriam, Morte D'Arthur*) is considered the greatest (elegy, novel, sonnet) in the English language.

26. In 1850 (Tennyson, Shelley, Wordsworth) was appointed poet laureate.

27. Lewis Carroll first told *Alice's Adventures in Wonderland* to (three women friends, the three Liddell daughters, two boys).

28. Sir Walter Scott maintained a position as a (legal official, sailor, history professor) throughout most of his life.

**Circle the letter of the lines that best answers the following questions** (each answer, 1 point).

29. In the Introduction to *Songs of Experience*, who is the reader told to listen to for spiritual guidance?

   a. the preacher of the Word of God
   b. the poet-prophet
   c. Jesus Christ
   d. The Experienced One

30. In the Preface to *Lyrical Ballads*, Wordsworth defined "good poetry" as?

   a. the ordered convenience of common place things
   b. the precise description of powerful feelings
   c. the spontaneous overflow of powerful feelings
   d. the careful description of feelings

31. William Blake's "two contrary states of the human soul" may be described as?

   a. a child-like vision of reality and an adult vision of reality
   b. an insane vision of reality and a sane vision of reality
   c. a spiritual vision of the world and a fleshly vision of the world
   d. a Christian view of the world and a mystical vision of reality

32. What historical conflict serves as the basis for *Ivanhoe*?

    a. The Norman and the French struggle for control of the throne of England
    b. The Norman and the Saxon struggle for control of the throne of England
    c. The Battle of Waterloo
    d. The Irish Conquest

33. Because the beliefs of the Tullivers and Dodsons, from *The Mill on the Floss*, are based upon unchanging traditions, their lives are characterized by?

    a. freedom                         c. oppressive narrowness
    b. beauty and truth                d. greatness and nobility

34. In *Apologia Pro Vita Sua*, John Newman compares the doctrine of Transubstantiation to that of he Trinity because?

    a. He is trying to establish the point that some religious doctrines cannot be explained intellectually though they are true.
    b. He believes that Thomas More invented both doctrines.
    c. He thinks that the doctrine of the Trinity is intellectually removed from doubt.
    d. Both doctrines can be proven by philosophical means.

35. Carlyle's new faith for a secular society did what?

    a. Allowed for a sense of religious awe yet did not dictate a standard of morality.
    b. Called all to repentance according to the Scriptures.
    c. Held all accountable to a universal standard of right and wrong.
    d. Trusted in the powers of reason to point man to the truth.

36. In *Sartor Resartus*, why does the professor say that Christianity in the Nineteenth Century is "lying in ruins, over grown with jungle?"

    a. It is the religion best suited for the modern man.
    b. It is useless now and needs to be replaced.
    c. It is teeming with life and vitality.
    d. It needs to be rebuilt.

37. In the Prologue of *In Memoriam*, Tennyson explains the differences between?

    a. faith and knowledge
    b. Protestantism and Roman Catholicism
    c. happiness and grief
    d. men and women

38. In section 96 of *In Memoriam*, Tennyson excuses his doubt of orthodox Christianity by calling it?

    a. deceiving doubt                 c. hurried doubt
    b. honest doubt                    d. rational doubt

39. In *The Pickwick Papers*, what is the stated purpose of the new branch of Pickwickians

    a. To conduct scientific experiments.
    b. To move to American and record accounts of its society.
    c. To discuss relevant political matters.
    d. To share accounts of their journeys and adventures.

40.  In "My Last Duchess," what is our only source of information about the duchess?

   a.  The duchess herself
   b.  The painting
   c.  The duke
   d.  The Count's messenger

41.  Known as the prince of English essayists, Charles Lamb's style is?

   a.  spontaneous with a romantic sensibility for nature's powers to stir the emotions
   b.  polished with a neoclassical attentions to the powers of reasons
   c.  polished and conversational with a romantic sensibility for the commonplace things and activities of London
   d.  spontaneous and unpolished

42.  What does Shelley ask the West Wind to do for him in Part V of "Ode to the West Wind?"

   a.  to make him god of the forest
   b.  to grant him relieve from the burden of sin and death
   c.  to allow him to remain on the ship
   d.  to make him a lyre, to be one with his spirit, give him new life, and make him a prophet of the West Wind's powers

**Fill in each of the blanks using items from the following word list** (each answer, 3 points).

| | | |
|---|---|---|
| *The Importance of Being Earnest* | imagination | relativity |
| *The Rime of the Ancient Mariner* | transcendental | historical |
| *The Ring and the Book* | Elizabeth Barrett | art |
| *Biographia Literaria* | Enlightenment | |

43.  Sir Walter Scott is the originator of the _____ novel.

44.  Coleridge encouraged Wordsworth to espouse _____ beliefs in his poetry.

45.  Byron's heroic figures were influential in shaping modern concepts of moral

   _____ .

46.  The publication of _____ in 1817, established Coleridge's reputation as the father of a new tradition of literary criticism.

47.  John Keats believe that _____ alone could elevate one's senses to the spiritual world.

48.  Shelley believed in the redeeming power of the _____ to effect a golder age of society.

49.  Intellectually, the Romantic Movement was based on the tenets of the _____ .

50.  The moral lesson of _____ is that there are spiritual blessings for those that love God's creation.

51.  In 1846 Browning married _____ and moved with her to Italy.

52.  The publication of _____ in 1868-9, elevated Browning's reputation as a poet above that of Tennyson.

53.  First performed in 1895, _____ is considered Wilde's masterpiece.

# BRITISH LITERATURE LIFEPAC FIVE ALTERNATE TEST

**Name** _____

**Date** _____

**Score** _____

75 / 94

**Fill in each of the blanks using items from the following word list** (each answer, 3 points).

Virginia Woolf                 Oxford                                          "Adam's Curse"
"Sailing to Byzantium"         stream of consciousness          C. S. Lewis
Irish                                Christian                                      socialism
victory                             "The Love Song of J. Alfred Prufrock"

1.  In her books and essays in support of the Women's Suffrage Movement,
    _____ articulated her belief that a society dominated by males will
    always lead to the oppression of women.

2.  Woolf's "new" style incorporated the _____ technique.

3.  The two great apologists for orthodox religion in the twentieth century were G. K.
    Chesterton and _____.

4.  At the outbreak of World War II, Lewis was asked to give a series of radio lectures on basic
    _____ beliefs.

5.  W.B. Yeats' first poems convey an interest in _____ folklore.

6.  George Bernard Shaw's main purpose in writing plays was to make
    _____ seem more appealing.

7.  According to Yeats' poem entitled _____ , the modern world thinks that
    creating poetry is worthless work.

8.  In _____ the narrator sails to Byzantium in order to escape the degra-
    dation of old age.

9.  The narrator's view of modern relationships in _____ is that they are
    empty and meaningless.

10. In his speech to the House of Commons on 13 May 1940, Churchill said that the aim of his
    administrations was _____ .

**Answer *true* or *false* for each of the following statements** (each answer, 2 points).

11. _____ In Virginia Woolf's story *The Duchess and the Jeweller*, Oliver Bacon is a middle
    class merchant who seeks the society of the upper class.

12. _____ Oliver has flashbacks to when he was a boy selling stolen dogs to fashionable
    women because his dealings with the duchess are very similar.

13. _____ In James Joyce's *Araby*, the boy goes to the bazaar because he wants to buy a
    gift for a girl that he is infatuated with.

14. _____ The boy doesn't buy anything at the bazaar because he doesn't have enough money.

15. _____ The boy eventually sees himself as a "creature driven and derided by vanity" because his effort to buy the girl resulted only in frustration and anger.

16. _____ "The absence of God" from society caused many to be optimistic about man's existence.

17. _____ The stream of consciousness technique attempts to tell a story through the natural flow of a character's thoughts.

18. _____ Joseph Conrad set his stories at sea and in foreign lands in order to supply a world removed from the influence of western civilization.

19. _____ After World War II, members of the ruling Labour Party cut benefits for the poor and lower class in order to pay for war debts owed to the United States.

20. _____ After Germany exceeded the limitations set forth by the Treaty of Versailles, Britain entered into an alliance with Italy to stop Hitler's advance across Europe.

21. _____ The First World War caused people to doubt the goodness of God and the goodness of technology.

22. _____ Britain refuses to grant Ireland total independence because many Protestants living in northern Ireland wish to remain under British rule.

23. _____ In Shaw's play Pygmalion, Professor Higgins behaves like a middle class gentleman to Eliza Doolittle.

24. _____ Alfred Doolittle comes to Higgins to demand the return of his daughter, Eliza.

**Circle the letter of the lines that best answers the following questions** (each answer, 2 points).

25. According to Huxley's *Brave New World*, how does Mustapha Mond think that God manifests himself to modern men?

    a.  In the Scriptures.         c.  In relationships.

    b.  In miracles.              d.  As an absence.

26. What does the Savage think makes man noble and heroic?

    a.  The absence of God.         c.  Belief in the existence of God.

    b.  Immoral behavior and desires.     d.  Romantic feelings.

27. In Chapter 10 of *The Screwtape Letters*, on what grounds does Screwtape encourage Wormwood to persuade the patient to maintain his new acquaintances?

    a.  That he might enjoy the pleasures of the world.

    b.  That he might learn the ways of the world.

    c.  That he is being a witness to them and to not associate with them would be "Puritanical."

    d.  That he might live in accordance to the Enemy's wishes.

28. In Chapter 20, Screwtape attributes the creation of fashionable sex types to demons. What is the purpose behind this cultural endeavor?

    a.  To wreck any chances of people having healthy marriages.

    b.  To perpetuate the existence of lust.

    c.  To distract people from praying for a mate.

    d.  To cause divorces to multiply.

29.    According to Hardy's poem, "The Respectable Burgher," why do the "Reverend Doctors" think that the stories which include supernatural events are included in the Bible?

    a.   The stories contain historical details not found anywhere else.

    b.   The stories add a romantic air to religion.

    c.   The stories are truthful.

    d.   The stories were inspired by the Holy Spirit.

30.    In *Heart of Darkness*, what are Kurtz's last words?

    a.   "The horror. The horror."

    b.   "My love. My love."

    c.   "Save me from this hell."

    d.   "The jungle is a dark, dark place."

31.    In "The Love Song of J. Alfred Prufrock," why does the narrator mean when he says, "I have measured out my life with coffee spoons?"

    a.   Every aspect of his life has great significance and meaning.

    b.   His life is full of trite acts that amount to nothing.

    c.   He trusts in God for every detail in his life.

    d.   Even the most mundane things have meaning and significance.

32.    According G. K. Chesterton's book *Orthodoxy*, what is the "natural fountain of revolution and reform?"

    a.   A skepticism of traditional moral and beliefs.

    b.   Liberal theology.

    c.   Atheism.

    d.   Old orthodoxy.

33.    In its context, explain Chesterton's statement: "Not only is the faith the mother of all worldly energies but its foes are the fathers of all worldly confusion."

    a.   Orthodox Christianity is the only true basis of liberty, humanity and love.

    b.   All religions supply a firm foundation for world peace.

    c.   Orthodox Christianity is not the only basis for liberty, humanity and love.

    d.   Religious beliefs have not impact on society.

34.    In *The Finest Hour speech*, what does Winston Churchill say is dependent upon Britain's victory?

    a.   The survival of materialism.

    b.   The survival of democracy.

    c.   The survival of Christian civilization.

    d.   The survival of Nazism.

**Underline the correct answer in each of the following statements** (each answer, 2 points).

35.    Joyce rebelled against the (Protestant, Roman Catholic, Muslim) beliefs of middle class society.

36.    In 1914 Joyce published (*A Portrait of the Artist as a Young Man*, *Ulysses*, *Dubliners*), a collection of short stories containing symbolic meanings of the modern world.

37. Aldous Huxley was the grandson of Thomas Huxley the champion of (Protestantism, Darwinism, mysticism).

38. (*Crome Yellow, Brave New World, Point Counter Point*) is a "satirical fantasy" set in seventh century AF (After [Henry] Ford) where humans are conditioned from conception to take their place in a caste system based on scientifically graded intelligence.

39. During the First World War, (G. K. Chesterton, C. S. Lewis, T. S. Eliot ) was asked to write pamphlets in support of England's efforts to stave off German aggression.

40. Winston Churchill's writing style can be characterized as (modern, grand, colloquial).

41. In his poetry written during the twentieth century, Hardy experimented with (verse forms, prose forms, dramatic monologues), using a language of the (upper class, common people, clergy).

A
N
S
W
E
R

K
E
Y
S

**Suggested Additional Reading for British Literature LIFEPAC 1**

*Le Morte d' Arthur* by Thomas Malory

"The Nun's Priest's Tale" from *The Canterbury Tales* by Geoffrey Chaucer

*The Reformation in England*, vol. 1 by J. H. Merle d'Aubigné

## SECTION ONE

| | |
|---|---|
| 1.1 | literature, honor, delightful. |
| 1.2 | background |
| 1.3 | modern |
| 1.4 | medieval |
| 1.5 | Rome, Renaissance |
| 1.6 | intellectual, spiritual |
| 1.7 | spiritual, intellectual |
| 1.8 | Old, Middle |
| 1.9 | Anglo-Saxons |
| 1.10 | Norman, French |
| 1.11 | dialects |
| 1.12 | dialect |
| 1.13 | Middle Ages |
| 1.14 | Angles, Saxons, Jutes |
| 1.15 | Paganism |
| 1.16 | Classical Paganism |
| 1.17 | Christianity |
| 1.18 | Christian, culture |
| 1.19 | heroic ideal |
| 1.20 | king |
| 1.21 | fame, oral |
| 1.22 | *Beowulf* |
| 1.23 | Greeks |
| 1.24 | Scops, Roman Catholic |
| 1.25 | Roman Catholicism |
| 1.26 | Scotland |
| 1.27 | Brude |
| 1.28 | Alfred |
| 1.29 | learning |
| 1.30 | Old English |
| 1.31 | Normans |
| 1.32 | France |
| 1.33 | Hastings |
| 1.34 | feudalism |
| 1.35 | king |
| 1.36 | French |
| 1.37 | common |
| 1.38 | Middle |
| 1.39 | France |
| 1.40 | romance |

| | |
|---|---|
| 1.41 | Middle Ages |
| 1.42 | Black |
| 1.43 | Roman Catholic Church |
| 1.44 | John Wycliffe |
| 1.45 | Reformation |
| 1.46 | plays |
| 1.47 | Mystery |
| 1.48 | Morality |
| 1.49 | piety |
| 1.50 | England |
| 1.51 | seven |
| 1.52 | astronomy |
| 1.53 | Christianity |
| 1.54 | Old English |
| 1.55 | oral-formulaic |
| 1.56 | God |
| 1.57 | T |
| 1.58 | F |
| 1.59 | T |
| 1.60 | F |
| 1.61 | F |
| 1.62 | F |
| 1.63 | F |
| 1.64 | T |
| 1.65 | T |
| 1.66 | F |
| 1.67 | T |
| 1.68 | F |
| 1.69 | T |
| 1.70 | F |
| 1.71 | F |
| 1.72 | T |
| 1.73 | T |
| 1.74 | T |
| 1.75 | T |
| 1.76 | F |
| 1.77 | F |
| 1.78 | T |
| 1.79 | T |
| 1.80 | T |
| 1.81 | T |
| 1.82 | Epic |
| 1.83 | West Midlands, pagan |
| 1.84 | Chaplain |
| 1.85 | Scandinavia |
| 1.86 | heroic |
| 1.87 | kenning |
| 1.88 | Christian |
| 1.89 | worldview |
| 1.90 | immortality |

1.91   F
1.92   T
1.93   T
1.94   T
1.95   T
1.96   T
1.97   T
1.98   F
1.99   T
1.100  T
1.101  F
1.102  F
1.103  T
1.104  T
1.105  F
1.106  T
1.107  F
1.108  T
1.109  T
1.110  F
1.111  F
1.112  T
1.113  T
1.114  F
1.115  T
1.116  T
1.117  T
1.118  F
1.119  T
1.120  T
1.121  F
1.122  T
1.123  F
1.124  F

**SECTION TWO**

| | |
|---|---|
| 2.1 | human |
| 2.2 | spiritual |
| 2.3 | middle |
| 2.4 | King Edward III |
| 2.5 | Parliament |
| 2.6 | characters |
| 2.7 | folly |
| 2.8 | Italian |
| 2.9 | English |
| 2.10 | four |
| 2.11 | Middle Ages |

| | |
|---|---|
| 2.12 | F |
| 2.13 | T |
| 2.14 | T |
| 2.15 | T |
| 2.16 | T |
| 2.17 | T |
| 2.18 | F |
| 2.19 | T |
| 2.20 | F |
| 2.21 | F |
| 2.22 | T |
| 2.23 | T |
| 2.24 | F |
| 2.25 | F |
| 2.26 | T |
| 2.27 | T |
| 2.28 | F |
| 2.29 | T |
| 2.30 | T |
| 2.31 | T |
| 2.32 | T |
| 2.33 | T |
| 2.34 | F |
| 2.35 | T |
| 2.36 | T |
| 2.37 | F |
| 2.38 | T |
| 2.39 | F |

| | |
|---|---|
| 2.40 | T |
| 2.41 | T |
| 2.42 | F |
| 2.43 | F |
| 2.44 | T |
| 2.45 | F |
| 2.46 | T |
| 2.47 | F |
| 2.48 | F |
| 2.49 | T |
| 2.50 | T |
| 2.51 | T |
| 2.52 | F |
| 2.53 | T |
| 2.54 | T |

| | |
|---|---|
| 2.55 | Church, reform |
| 2.56 | society |
| 2.57 | 1372 |
| 2.58 | William Langland |
| 2.59 | commoners |
| 2.60 | neighbor |
| 2.61 | visions, allegory |
| 2.62 | history |

| | |
|---|---|
| 2.63 | F |
| 2.64 | T |
| 2.65 | F |
| 2.66 | T |
| 2.67 | F |
| 2.68 | T |
| 2.69 | T |
| 2.70 | T |
| 2.71 | F |
| 2.72 | F |
| 2.73 | T |
| 2.74 | T |
| 2.75 | F |
| 2.76 | T |

**SECTION THREE**

| | | | |
|---|---|---|---|
| 3.1 | morality | 3.25 | T |
| 3.2 | Mystery | 3.26 | F |
| 3.3 | Moralities | 3.27 | T |
| 3.4 | Moralities | 3.28 | T |
| 3.5 | Roman Catholic | 3.29 | T |
| 3.6 | good deeds | 3.30 | F |
| | | 3.31 | T |
| 3.7 | T | 3.32 | F |
| 3.8 | F | 3.33 | F |
| 3.9 | F | 3.34 | F |
| 3.10 | T | 3.35 | F |
| 3.11 | T | 3.36 | T |
| 3.12 | T | 3.37 | F |
| 3.13 | T | 3.38 | T |
| 3.14 | F | 3.39 | F |
| 3.15 | F | 3.40 | T |
| 3.16 | F | 3.41 | T |
| | | 3.42 | T |
| 3.17 | Lancastrian | 3.43 | F |
| 3.18 | Yorkist | 3.44 | T |
| 3.19 | *Le Morte d' Arthur* | 3.45 | F |
| 3.20 | King Arthur | 3.46 | F |
| 3.21 | knight | 3.47 | T |
| 3.22 | William Caxton | 3.48 | F |
| 3.23 | fails, Guenevere | 3.49 | F |
| 3.24 | destroy | 3.50 | F |
| | | 3.51 | T |

**Suggested Additional Reading for British Literature LIFEPAC 2**

*Fierce Wars and Faithful Loves: Spenser's Faerie Queen, Book 1* by Roy Maynard (This is a modernized version of Spenser's work with helpful annotations.)

*Foxe's Book of Martyrs* by John Foxe

*The Reformation in England*, vol. 2 by J.H. Merle d'Aubigné

## SECTION ONE

| | |
|---|---|
| 1.1 | Reformation |
| 1.2 | Word of God |
| 1.3 | Renaissance |
| 1.4 | Renaissance |
| 1.5 | Oxford Reformers |
| 1.6 | Humanists |
| 1.7 | human reason |
| 1.8 | human reason |
| 1.9 | church |
| 1.10 | Scripture |
| 1.11 | Reformation |
| 1.12 | learned |
| 1.13 | William Tyndale |
| 1.14 | condemned |
| 1.15 | Scripture |
| 1.16 | refused, Head |
| 1.17 | Catholic |
| 1.18 | dissolved |
| 1.19 | authorized |
| 1.20 | The Great |
| 1.21 | Edward VI |
| 1.22 | Protestant |
| 1.23 | reverse |
| 1.24 | Protestants |
| 1.25 | Europe |
| 1.26 | Anglican |
| 1.27 | biblical |
| 1.28 | middle |
| 1.29 | independent, nations |
| 1.30 | English |
| 1.31 | sonnet |
| 1.32 | fourteen |
| 1.33 | English |
| 1.34 | epic |
| 1.35 | pastoral |
| 1.36 | Seneca, classical, horror |
| 1.37 | English history |
| 1.38 | tragedy |
| 1.39 | nobleman |
| 1.40 | men and boys |
| 1.41 | Public theaters |

| | |
|---|---|
| 1.42 | oval |
| 1.43 | grace |
| 1.44 | Elizabethan |
| 1.45 | law |
| 1.46 | self-affliction |
| 1.47 | Lord Chancellor |
| 1.48 | Latin |
| 1.49 | *Utopia* |
| 1.50 | reason |
| 1.51 | no place |
| 1.52 | Tyndale |
| 1.53 | treason, Henry VIII |
| 1.54 | T |
| 1.55 | F |
| 1.56 | T |
| 1.57 | F |
| 1.58 | F |
| 1.59 | T |
| 1.60 | T |
| 1.61 | F |
| 1.62 | T |
| 1.63 | F |
| 1.64 | T |
| 1.65 | T |
| 1.66 | F |
| 1.67 | T |
| 1.68 | Scripture |
| 1.69 | Greek |
| 1.70 | tutor |
| 1.71 | Elizabeth |
| 1.72 | *The Schoolmaster* |
| 1.73 | beating |
| 1.74 | encouragement |
| 1.75 | immoral |
| 1.76 | T |
| 1.77 | F |
| 1.78 | F |
| 1.79 | T |
| 1.80 | F |
| 1.81 | F |
| 1.82 | T |
| 1.83 | T |
| 1.84 | T |
| 1.85 | T |
| 1.86 | T |
| 1.87 | F |
| 1.88 | T |
| 1.89 | F |
| 1.90 | T |
| 1.91 | T |
| 1.92 | T |
| 1.93 | T |

| | | | |
|---|---|---|---|
| 1.94 | Oxford, Greek, final | 1.122 | F |
| 1.95 | tutor | 1.123 | T |
| 1.96 | Edward VI's | 1.124 | F |
| 1.97 | persecutions, Roman Catholic | 1.125 | T |
| 1.98 | England | 1.126 | F |
| 1.99 | English | 1.127 | T |
| 1.100 | *Acts and Monuments* | 1.128 | T |
| 1.101 | 6000 | 1.129 | T |
| 1.102 | church | 1.130 | F |
| 1.103 | historical, evangelicalism, biblical | 1.131 | F |
| | | 1.132 | T |
| 1.104 | T | 1.133 | T |
| 1.105 | F | 1.134 | T |
| 1.106 | T | | |
| 1.107 | T | | |
| 1.108 | F | | |
| 1.109 | F | | |
| 1.110 | T | | |
| 1.111 | T | | |
| 1.112 | T | | |
| 1.113 | T | | |
| 1.114 | F | | |
| 1.115 | F | | |
| 1.116 | T | | |
| 1.117 | F | | |
| 1.118 | T | | |
| 1.119 | T | | |
| 1.120 | F | | |
| 1.121 | T | | |

## SECTION TWO

| | |
|---|---|
| 2.1 | Henry VIII |
| 2.2 | Cambridge |
| 2.3 | England |
| 2.4 | Petrarchian |
| 2.5 | conceit |
| 2.6 | Italian, 14, octave |
| 2.7 | question, sestet |
| 2.8 | rhythm |
| 2.9 | iambic |
| 2.10 | 5, line |
| 2.11 | sestet |
| 2.12 | 3 |
| 2.13 | English |

| | |
|---|---|
| 2.14 | T |
| 2.15 | T |
| 2.16 | F |
| 2.17 | T |
| 2.18 | T |
| 2.19 | F |
| 2.20 | F |
| 2.21 | F |
| 2.22 | T |
| 2.23 | F |
| 2.24 | F |
| 2.25 | T |
| 2.26 | T |
| 2.27 | F |
| 2.28 | F |
| 2.29 | F |

| | |
|---|---|
| 2.30 | Ireland |
| 2.31 | Oxford |
| 2.32 | Paris |
| 2.33 | Cupbearer |
| 2.34 | Queen Elizabeth |
| 2.35 | Catholic |
| 2.36 | pastoral romance |
| 2.37 | *Old Arcadia* |
| 2.38 | sonnet sequence |
| 2.39 | sonnet sequence |
| 2.40 | *Astrophil and Stella* |
| 2.41 | *The Defense of Posey* |
| 2.42 | mortally |
| 2.43 | courtier |

| | |
|---|---|
| 2.44 | T |
| 2.45 | F |
| 2.46 | T |
| 2.47 | F |
| 2.48 | T |
| 2.49 | F |
| 2.50 | F |

| | |
|---|---|
| 2.51 | T |
| 2.52 | F |
| 2.53 | T |
| 2.54 | T |
| 2.55 | F |
| 2.56 | T |
| 2.57 | T |
| 2.58 | T |
| 2.59 | T |
| 2.60 | T |
| 2.61 | F |
| 2.62 | T |
| 2.63 | T |

| | |
|---|---|
| 2.64 | middle |
| 2.65 | Richard Mulcaster |
| 2.66 | Cambridge |
| 2.67 | Master's degree |
| 2.68 | eclogue |
| 2.69 | Chaucer |
| 2.70 | verse |
| 2.71 | Sir Philip Sidney |
| 2.72 | Irish |
| 2.73 | Sir Walter Raleigh |
| 2.74 | "Amoretti" |
| 2.75 | archaic, chivalry |
| 2.76 | Revelation |
| 2.77 | Queen Elizabeth |
| 2.78 | Chaucer, Westminster |

| | |
|---|---|
| 2.79 | F |
| 2.80 | T |
| 2.81 | T |
| 2.82 | F |
| 2.83 | F |
| 2.84 | T |
| 2.85 | T |
| 2.86 | F |
| 2.87 | T |
| 2.88 | T |
| 2.89 | F |
| 2.90 | T |
| 2.91 | F |
| 2.92 | T |
| 2.93 | T |
| 2.94 | T |
| 2.95 | T |
| 2.96 | F |
| 2.97 | T |
| 2.98 | T |
| 2.99 | F |
| 2.100 | F |
| 2.101 | T |

2.102   poets, musicians
2.103   Sir Philip Sidney
2.104   "Arcadia"
2.105   divine
2.106   verse, meter
2.107   author, men
2.108   religion, arts
2.109   wanting
2.110   Falsehood, rejected, loves
2.111   mischief
2.112   olive
2.113   trust
2.114   dust
2.115   truth, lies
2.116   snake
2.117   melt
2.118   feet
2.119   judges

**SECTION THREE**

| | |
|---|---|
| 3.1 | Oxford |
| 3.2 | poet |
| 3.3 | Huguenots |
| 3.4 | Virginia |
| 3.5 | Queen's guard |
| 3.6 | Queen Elizabeth's |
| 3.7 | King James |
| 3.8 | prison |
| 3.9 | gold |
| 3.10 | beheaded |

| | |
|---|---|
| 3.11 | T |
| 3.12 | F |
| 3.13 | T |
| 3.14 | F |
| 3.15 | T |
| 3.16 | T |
| 3.17 | T |
| 3.18 | T |
| 3.19 | F |
| 3.20 | T |
| 3.21 | F |
| 3.22 | F |
| 3.23 | T |
| 3.24 | F |
| 3.25 | T |

| | |
|---|---|
| 3.26 | Stratford-on-Avon |
| 3.27 | Anne Hathaway |
| 3.28 | three |
| 3.29 | playwright |
| 3.30 | Lord Chamberlain's Men |
| 3.31 | narrative poem |
| 3.32 | coat of arms |
| 3.33 | New Place |
| 3.34 | romantic |
| 3.35 | three |
| 3.36 | Shakespearean |
| 3.37 | Globe |
| 3.38 | fall, redemption |
| 3.39 | 1623, *First* |
| 3.40 | First Folio |
| 3.41 | four |
| 3.42 | experimentation |
| 3.43 | second |
| 3.44 | tragedies |
| 3.45 | tragicomedy |
| 3.46 | ever-fixed |
| 3.47 | Love |
| 3.48 | loved |
| 3.49 | roses |
| 3.50 | Music |
| 3.51 | rare |

| | |
|---|---|
| 3.52 | F |
| 3.53 | T |
| 3.54 | T |
| 3.55 | T |
| 3.56 | F |
| 3.57 | T |
| 3.58 | T |
| 3.59 | F |
| 3.60 | F |
| 3.61 | F |
| 3.62 | F |
| 3.63 | F |
| 3.64 | T |
| 3.65 | F |
| 3.66 | F |
| 3.67 | T |
| 3.68 | T |
| 3.69 | T |
| 3.70 | F |
| 3.71 | T |
| 3.72 | T |
| 3.73 | T |
| 3.74 | F |
| 3.75 | T |
| 3.76 | T |
| 3.77 | F |
| 3.78 | F |
| 3.79 | F |
| 3.80 | T |
| 3.81 | T |
| 3.82 | T |
| 3.83 | T |
| 3.84 | F |
| 3.85 | T |
| 3.86 | F |
| 3.87 | T |
| 3.88 | F |
| 3.89 | F |
| 3.90 | F |
| 3.91 | T |
| 3.92 | F |
| 3.93 | F |
| 3.94 | F |
| 3.95 | F |
| 3.96 | F |
| 3.97 | T |
| 3.98 | T |

| | |
|---|---|
| 3.99 | Reformation |
| 3.100 | Latin Vulgate |
| 3.101 | *repent* |
| 3.102 | Greek and Hebrew |
| 3.103 | Tyndale's |

3.104   translating the Bible
3.105   English
3.106   Tyndale's
3.107   Geneva Bible
3.108   Geneva Bible
3.109   Geneva Bible
3.110   Queen Elizabeth
3.111   Latin Vulgate
3.112   Authorized Version
3.113   Geneva Bible
3.114   King James Version
3.115   King James Version, people
3.116   punishment
3.117   notwithstanding
3.118   plagued, humbled
3.119   leper
3.120   Geneva

**Suggested Additional Reading for British Literature LIFEPAC 3**

*The Great Christian Revolution* by Otto Scott

*Gulliver's Travels* by Jonathan Swift (full text)

*Pilgrim's Progress* by John Bunyan (full text)

*The Puritans* by D. Martin Lloyd-Jones

*Worldly Saints: The Puritans as They Really Were* by Leland Ryken

**SECTION ONE**

| | |
|---|---|
| 1.1 | F |
| 1.2 | T |
| 1.3 | F |
| 1.4 | F |
| 1.5 | T |
| 1.6 | F |
| 1.7 | T |
| 1.8 | T |
| 1.9 | T |
| 1.10 | T |
| 1.11 | T |
| 1.12 | F |
| 1.13 | T |
| 1.14 | T |
| 1.15 | T |

| | |
|---|---|
| 1.16 | Roman Catholicism |
| 1.17 | Anne More |
| 1.18 | preacher |
| 1.19 | Royal Chaplain, Lincoln's Inn |
| 1.20 | metaphysical |
| 1.21 | Jack Donne, Dr. John Donne |
| 1.22 | Puritan |

| | |
|---|---|
| 1.23 | b |
| 1.24 | c |
| 1.25 | a |
| 1.26 | c |
| 1.27 | a |
| 1.28 | b |
| 1.29 | c |
| 1.30 | b |
| 1.31 | c |

| | |
|---|---|
| 1.32 | Westminster School |
| 1.33 | playwright |
| 1.34 | William Shakespeare |
| 1.35 | benefit of clergy |
| 1.36 | masques |
| 1.37 | Cavalier |
| 1.38 | forms |
| 1.39 | neoclassical |

1.40 His thoughts and affections live on in his works.

1.41 The appeal and greatness of his work transcends the boundaries of time and culture.

1.42 Even a gifted poet must develop his talent for it to be good.

1.43 A kiss from his beloved.

1.44 The smell of his beloved.

1.45 The poet's statement that he swears that the wreath continues to grow after his beloved has breathed on it hints that he is not being serious. The image is a little ridiculous. Jonson is poking fun at the elaborate conceits found in Petrarchian sonnets.

| | |
|---|---|
| 1.46 | Cambridge |
| 1.47 | Member of Parliament |
| 1.48 | minister |
| 1.49 | holy |
| 1.50 | Anglican |
| 1.51 | poetry |
| 1.52 | innovative |
| 1.53 | metaphysical |

1.54 The poem's form reinforces the message that we need the Lord's help to be delivered from sin.

1.55 The poet is morally unable to overcome the corruption of sin and death.

1.56 The poem's form reinforces the message that our broken, humbled hearts are the "altars" upon which we are to offer our sacrifices of praise to God.

1.57 His heart and tears.

1.58 His heart is broken.

1.59 God

**SECTION TWO**

| | |
|---|---|
| 2.1 | Renaissance |
| 2.2 | Church of England |
| 2.3 | six |
| 2.4 | Parliamentary supporter |
| 2.5 | Independent |
| 2.6 | Oliver Cromwell |
| 2.7 | *Paradise Lost* |

| | |
|---|---|
| 2.8 | b |
| 2.9 | d |
| 2.10 | a |
| 2.11 | b |
| 2.12 | a |
| 2.13 | c |
| 2.14 | d |
| 2.15 | c |
| 2.16 | b |
| 2.17 | b |

| | |
|---|---|
| 2.18 | Puritan |
| 2.19 | Oxford |
| 2.20 | Laud, God's Word |
| 2.21 | Rump, Oliver Cromwell |
| 2.22 | Harvard |
| 2.23 | Scripture |

| | |
|---|---|
| 2.24 | b |
| 2.25 | a |
| 2.26 | d |
| 2.27 | b |
| 2.28 | d |
| 2.29 | a |
| 2.30 | c |
| 2.31 | b |
| 2.32 | a |
| 2.33 | b |

| | |
|---|---|
| 2.34 | physical |
| 2.35 | scientific |
| 2.36 | law |
| 2.37 | James I |
| 2.38 | bribes |

2.39 *Essays or Counsels, Civil and Moral*

2.40 *Novum Organum*

2.41 The kind that "sinketh in, and settleth" in the mind.

2.42 The inquiry, the knowledge and the belief of truth.

2.43 It will bring shame and dishonor on him.

2.44 A lie makes a man bold in his sin before God yet makes him a coward before men.

2.45 Private delight, ornament, and increased mental ability.

2.46 To "weight and consider."

2.47 A. "tasted"–to read only part of a book.
B. "swallowed"–to read a book but not intently.
C. "chewed and digested"–to read an entire book with diligence and attention.

## SECTION THREE

| | | | | |
|---|---|---|---|---|
| 3.1 | T | | 3.39 | tinker |
| 3.2 | F | | 3.40 | preaching |
| 3.3 | F | | 3.41 | John Owen |
| 3.4 | F | | 3.42 | Authorized |
| 3.5 | F | | 3.43 | Bible |
| 3.6 | T | | 3.44 | Grace Abounding to the Chief of Sinners |
| 3.7 | F | | | |
| 3.8 | T | | 3.45 | a |
| 3.9 | T | | 3.46 | d |
| 3.10 | T | | 3.47 | a |
| 3.11 | F | | 3.48 | c |
| 3.12 | T | | 3.49 | d |
| 3.13 | T | | 3.50 | a |
| 3.14 | T | | 3.51 | b |
| 3.15 | T | | 3.52 | d |
| 3.16 | T | | 3.53 | b |
| 3.17 | T | | 3.54 | a |
| 3.18 | T | | 3.55 | b |
| 3.19 | F | | 3.56 | a |
| 3.20 | F | | 3.57 | b |
| | | | 3.58 | c |
| | | | 3.59 | d |
| | | | 3.60 | b |
| | | | 3.61 | c |
| | | | 3.62 | d |

3.21 Cambridge

3.22 Royalist

3.23 poet laureate

3.24 occasional

3.25 Roman Catholic

3.26 translated

3.27 Neoclassical

3.28 Fear and uncertainty

3.29 Their principles upon which they stood were foolishness and only produced division and chaos.

3.30 David was chosen by God to rule Israel.

3.31 The rule of Charles II

3.32 The reestablishment of Charles II's authority and rule by official decree, and not by war, has brought peace and happiness to the nation. This line offers another perspective on the saying, "The pen is mightier than the sword."

3.33 Greed and lust for power. See lines 190-200.

3.34 Repentant. See lines 254 and 255.

3.35 Almost Christ-like power and honor. He is presented as God's chosen deliverer. See lines 250-323.

3.36 allegories

3.37 Parliamentary

3.38 *The Plain Man's Pathway to Heaven, The Practice of Piety*

3.63 prose

3.64 Ireland

3.65 Sir William Temple, Dublin

3.66 satirist

3.67 Enlightenment

3.68 Tory

3.69 a lady friend

3.70 Irish

3.71 Dean of St. Patrick's Cathedral

3.72 human wisdom

3.73 Well-read, middle-class doctor who holds an Enlightenment outlook on the world.

3.74 He was shipped wrecked while on a voyage to the East Indies.

3.75 The Lilliputians are only six inches tall.

3.76 The Tories, which favored the principles and practices of the High Church, are satirized as wearing high-heeled shoes. The Whigs, which favored the principles and practices of the Low Church, are satirized as wearing low-heeled shoes.

3.77 He characterizes their differences as nothing more than differing opinions on which end of an egg to break open.

3.78    It assumes that people are good at heart.

3.79    Children from birth are sent to be educated by public nurseries which prepare them for a life that befits their parents' rank, their own capacities, and their own inclinations.

3.80    To prepare them properly for their station in life.

3.81    Greek, Roman

3.82    Roman Catholic

3.83    William Wycherley

3.84    Scriblerus

3.85    Homer, Shakespeare

3.86    Satires

3.87    *An Essay on Man*

3.88    man

3.89    heroic

3.90    vindicate

3.91    To "vindicate the ways of God to man" by examining the world around them.

3.92    According to lines 17–20, man's knowledge is limited to the revelation of Nature. Therefore, knowledge of the supernatural or spiritual can only be derived from the physical universe. The poet does not acknowledge the Scriptures as a reliable source of divine knowledge.

3.93    Whatever we think might be wrong or unjust is ultimately right and good in because God ordained it.

3.94    To say that man is imperfect is to fault God's wisdom. Man is as he should be.

3.95    Pride

3.96    God is the first cause behind all the movements of the universe.

3.97    His submission to the God's will.

3.98    Whatever God has ordained to happen is ultimately right and good.

3.99    Pope states in the last stanza that "the proper study of mankind is man." Man's knowledge of himself is, therefore, limited to the powers of reason and natural revelation. Divine revelation is not to be consulted.

3.100   Scripture says that there is no one that is righteous in and of themselves. Nor is there anyone that seeks for God. Apart from God, we are all liars and do not like the truth. Therefore, how can man who is corrupted by sin be the "sole judge of truth?" God's Word is the "sole judge of truth" (2 Timothy 3:16).

3.101   hymns, hymnody

3.102   Neoclassical

3.103   Mr. Rowe's academy

3.104   Congregational

3.105   Sir John Abney

3.106   logic

3.107   Doctor of Divinity

3.108   children

3.109   Reformed

3.110   New Testament grace

3.111   Because Christ has come to redeem the world from sin.

3.112   The glories of His righteousness and wonders of His love.

3.113   God, the Almighty, gave His perfect Son for unworthy sinners.

3.114   Gratitude

3.115   What duties we owe to God.

3.116   Hope.

3.117   He is the only One that can help us.

3.118   Their strength only lasts for a season and soon fades.

3.119   Study, meditate, and love the Word of God.

3.120   God's Word

**Suggested Additional Reading for British Literature LIFEPAC 4**

*Alice in Wonderland* by Lewis Carroll
*Ivanhoe* by Sir Walter Scott
*The Pickwick Papers* by Charles Dickens
*Pride and Prejudice* by Jane Austen

## SECTION ONE

1.1 T
1.2 F
1.3 T
1.4 T
1.5 F
1.6 F
1.7 F
1.8 F
1.9 T
1.10 F
1.11 T
1.12 T
1.13 F
1.14 T
1.15 F
1.16 T
1.17 T
1.18 F

1.19 engraver
1.20 traditional
1.21 mysticism
1.22 symbolically
1.23 books
1.24 Scripture
1.25 illustrator
1.26 insane

1.27 a child-like vision of reality and an adult vision of reality

1.28 happy

1.29 a lamb

1.30 a child

1.31 Jesus Christ/goodness, purity and innocence

1.32 The poet-prophet

1.33 evil

1.34 "Who made thee?"

1.35 He does not answer it directly but implies that God, the Creator of the Lamb could not also be the Creator of evil or Satan.

1.36 a chapel

1.37 formalized religion or the visible church

1.38 The ministers of organized religion

1.39 It stifled or limited the expression of "true" spirituality.

1.40 Cambridge, French
1.41 sister, Samuel Taylor Coleridge
1.42 *Lyrical Ballads*
1.43 Romanticism
1.44 Lake District
1.45 *Poems in Two Volumes*
1.46 poet laureate
1.47 *The Prelude*
1.48 nature, Victorian

1.49 in an unusual way

1.50 Because "in that condition, the essential passions of the heart" can be communicated in the most natural way which is simple and emphatic in manner yet with force.

1.51 "the spontaneous overflow of powerful feelings"

1.52 "emotion recollected in tranquility"

1.53 "a dull and endless strife"

1.54 nature

1.55 "misshapes"

1.56 excitement, joy, wonder

1.57 He does not acknowledge God as the Creator of the universe.

1.58 d
1.59 a
1.60 c
1.61 b
1.62 c
1.63 d
1.64 c
1.65 b
1.66 a
1.67 b

1.68 The sailor tells his tale to a passer-by because he is compelled by his need for peace within his soul.

1.69 He kills an albatross for no reason.

1.70 They die of thirst

1.71 the curse of death

1.72 the burden of his guilt

1.73    his blessing of God's creatures

1.74    They are "inspirited" and able to perform their duties though dead.

1.75    the hermit

1.76    The presence of "goodly company" is the fruit of his peace with God's creation.

1.77    There are great spiritual blessings for those who love God's creation.

1.78    Scotland
1.79    historical
1.80    law, lawyer
1.81    legal official
1.82    romantic
1.83    businessman and a poet
1.84    Byron
1.85    novels
1.86    copyrights

1.87    Brian de Bois-Guilbert and the Disinherited Knight

1.88    Lady Rowena

1.89    The Disinherited Knight refused to reveal his identity and won the previous tournament.

1.90    the Black Knight

1.91    The tournament marshals remove Ivanhoe's helmet so that Lady Rowena may properly bestow upon him the chaplet.

1.92    He is wounded in his side.

1.93    the clothing, armor and formality used at a tournament of knights

1.94    the Black Knight

1.95    Normans and the Saxons

**SECTION TWO**

2.1    a
2.2    b
2.3    b
2.4    a
2.5    b
2.6    d

2.7    It is ironic because a single man in posses-
       sion of a good fortune is never lacking of
       available women wanting to become his wife.

2.8    She is irrational and often over reacts.
       He is calm and reserved.

2.9    She thinks that he has not talked to
       Mr. Bingly yet.

2.10   She is more concerned about the outworking
       of reason and truth rather than the inner
       workings of the heart which can be subjec-
       tively interpreted.

2.11   Mr. Darcy is aloof and cold. Mr. Bingly is
       warm and friendly to all.

2.12   Mr. Darcy refuses to dance with Elizabeth
       Bennet because he does not find her attrac-
       tive enough to do so.

2.13   The initial meeting of Elizabeth Bennet and
       Mr. Darcy differ from other romance stories
       in that they do not immediately fall in love.

2.14   c
2.15   a
2.16   b
2.17   b
2.18   c

2.19   It illustrates the emotional or romantically
       driven desire for china as opposed to a want
       based upon reason.

2.20   subjectively

2.21   so that they can be happier

2.22   The speaker responds to Bridget by saying
       that it is good that they have more money
       now because they are older and in need of
       more comfort that only wealth can provide.

2.23   As young people they could get along easier
       with less. For older people, happiness is
       directly related to comfort.

2.24   Elia presents the more rational answer to
       their situation. He understands and accepts
       the fact that age has altered their needs. The
       happiness of youth is not always the happi-
       ness of old age. (Answers might vary.)

2.25   A love for the past, like a love for china, is not
       dependent upon reason alone. It is based
       upon individual feelings and experiences.

2.26   It rambles in places and flows like a conver-
       sation.

2.27   *Hours of Idleness*
2.28   *Childe Harold's Pilgrimage*
2.29   England
2.30   Geneva
2.31   *Don Juan*
2.32   Greece
2.33   relativity

2.34   (Answer will vary.)
2.35   the "sultry" or warm climate

2.36   that pleasure is a sin, and sin is sometimes a
       pleasure

2.37   As a symbol of conventional morality, Don
       Alphonso, the husband, is presented as a
       frustrated idiot that cannot keep his wife
       from having an adulterous affair in his own
       household.

2.38   in Donna Julia's bed

2.39   So that people will know that it is an epic.

2.40   upper

2.41   "The Necessity of Atheism"
2.42   *Address to the Irish People*
2.43   Mary Godwin
2.44   Italy
2.45   "Pisan," "Ode to the West Wind"
2.46   romantic
2.47   imagination

2.48   b
2.49   a
2.50   a
2.51   b
2.52   c
2.53   a
2.54   b
2.55   d
2.56   c

2.57   surgeon-apothecary
2.58   Edmund Spenser
2.59   Leigh Hunt
2.60   *Endymion*
2.61   1819
2.62   *Lamia, Isabella, The Eve of St. Agnes, and Other Poems*
2.63   "The Fall of Hyperion"
2.64   Fanny Bawne
2.65   tuberculosis
2.66   Shakespeare
2.67   art
2.68   truth, beauty
2.69   a Grecian urn

2.70   The silent melodies of the musicians on the urn are sweeter because they never end. The music is played on forever in the minds of those that look at the urn and imagine.

2.71   As a work of art, he is 'frozen' on the surface of the urn.

2.72   no

2.73   It never fades.

2.74   They are a work of art, and therefore unchanging.

2.75   The urn, as a work of art, teases mortal humans by making them hope that their happiness will last as long as the happiness of the figures on the urn.

2.76   The ultimate reality or truth that we need to know on earth is that "Beauty is truth, truth beauty."

**SECTION THREE**

| | |
|---|---|
| 3.1 | T |
| 3.2 | T |
| 3.3 | F |
| 3.4 | F |
| 3.5 | T |
| 3.6 | T |
| 3.7 | F |
| 3.8 | T |
| 3.9 | T |
| 3.10 | F |
| 3.11 | T |
| 3.12 | T |
| 3.13 | F |
| 3.14 | F |
| 3.15 | T |
| 3.16 | T |
| 3.17 | b |
| 3.18 | c |
| 3.19 | d |
| 3.20 | a |
| 3.21 | c |
| 3.22 | a |
| 3.23 | b |
| 3.24 | a |
| 3.25 | b |
| 3.26 | a |

3.27    Love of God

3.28    the Godlike that is in man

3.29    It is useless now and needs to be replaced.

3.30    He states that the professor's character is questionable and that he makes strange comments.

3.31    It has changed much over the centuries, but its changes have helped the people little.

3.32    his religious feelings

3.33    The professor claims that God speaks to him directly. Therefore, since his bible is in his heart, no one can test its authenticity.

| | |
|---|---|
| 3.34 | F |
| 3.35 | T |
| 3.36 | F |
| 3.37 | T |
| 3.38 | F |
| 3.39 | T |
| 3.40 | T |
| 3.41 | F |
| 3.42 | T |
| 3.43 | F |
| 3.44 | b |
| 3.45 | c |
| 3.46 | a |
| 3.47 | b |
| 3.48 | a |
| 3.49 | b |

3.50    clergyman

3.51    *Poems, Chiefly Lyrical*

3.52    Arthur Hallam, ten

3.53    *Poems*

3.54    *In Memoriam*, elegy

3.55    poet laureate

3.56    *Idylls of the King*

3.57    classical

3.58    transcendentalism

3.59    Faith is not based upon knowledge but bridges the gap of belief where knowledge is deficient. Faith is not needed where knowledge abounds.

3.60    He sees himself as an infant, limited in knowledge and helplessly dependent upon God for truth.

3.61    Science or nature gives a darkened picture of reality that faith urges us to believe.

3.62    His thoughts and being come alive through the reading of a letter.

3.63    doubt

3.64    He calls it "honest doubt," implying that doubt of truth is better than belief in that which is false.

3.65    the feelings of his heart

3.66    He has become "mix'd" with God and Nature."

3.67    spiritual truth, truths that cannot be discovered through scientific experiments

3.68    factory, unpaid debts

3.69    reporter

3.70    *Sketches by Boz*

3.71    *The Pickwick Papers*

3.72    Catherine Hogarth

3.73    America, abolition of slavery

3.74    Christmas books

3.75    theatrical company, theater

3.76    editor

3.77    *All the Year Round*

3.78    public readings of his works

3.79    to share accounts of their journeys and adventures

3.80 Mr. Pickwick is an intelligent, dignified and eloquent man that is sure of himself and his opinions. In appearance he is plump and bald-headed and wears glasses.

3.81 She is his landlady.

3.82 to marry him

3.83 According to Victorian standards, it gives appearance of a very intimate relationship.

3.84 He tries to avenge his mother's apparent hurt and strikes Mr. Pickwick repeatedly.

3.85 Sam Weller is a man-servant that Mr. Pickwick is interested in hiring.

3.86 theism

3.87 tutors

3.88 "Paracelsus"

3.89 *Dramatic Lyrics*

3.90 Elizabeth Barrett

3.91 *Men and Women*

3.92 1861

3.93 *The Ring and the Book*

3.94 1881, Oxford

3.95 Romantics

3.96 dignified nobleman

3.97 a portrait of his last wife

3.98 an artist

3.99 She did not value the good name he had given her above anything else that she loved.

3.100 (Answers will vary)

3.101 the duke

3.102 the count's servant

3.103 line 45

3.104 to arrange another marriage for the duke

3.105 b

3.106 a

3.107 b

3.108 d

3.109 c

3.110 b

3.111 a

3.112 b

3.113 a

3.114 c

3.115 a

3.116 c

3.117 b

3.118 a

3.119 c

3.120 Aesthetic, for art's sake.

3.121 Walter Pater

3.122 America

3.123 *Vera, or the Nihilists*

3.124 Constance Lloyd

3.125 1891

3.126 *The Importance of Being Earnest*

3.127 experience

3.128 *De Profundis*

3.129 Roman Catholicism

3.130 Aunt Augusta and Gwendolen

3.131 because Aunt Augusta does not like him

3.132 When one proposes, one might get accepted and then all the excitement will be over.

3.133 He is Gwendolen's cousin.

3.134 She is his aunt.

3.135 He adopts another name so that he can come and go as he pleases.

3.136 Because he has invented an imaginary brother so that he can go to town as often as he likes.

3.137 Jack's imaginary brother.

3.138 The name Ernest produces the right vibrations, which inspire absolute confidence.

3.139 He wishes to be "earnest" with Gwendolen so that he can marry her.

3.140 Jack is not entirely truthful with Gwendolen about his true identity. He proposes to Gwendolen as Ernest, but he is really Jack. He, in fact, is not earnest or Ernest. Gwendolen's desire to marry a man named Ernest is entirely shallow. There is nothing truly serious about her desire to marry him.

3.141 clergyman

3.142 mathematics

3.143 symbolic logic

3.144 the three Liddell daughters

3.145 *Through the Looking Glass*

3.146 The gardeners are painting the roses red because the are afraid that the Queen will cut off their heads if the roses are white.

3.147 playing cards

3.148 croquet

3.149 It is made up of living things that never stay still.

3.150 Alice is afraid that she will incur the Queen's wrath and get her head cut off.

3.151 The Cheshire-Cat.

3.152 No one plays by the rules.

3.153 She threatens to cut off people's heads.

**Suggested Additional Reading for British Literature LIFEPAC 5**

*Orthodoxy* by G. K. Chesterton

*Four Quartets* by T. S. Eliot

*The Chronicles of Narnia* by C. S. Lewis

*The Screwtape Letters* by C. S. Lewis

**SECTION ONE**

| | |
|---|---|
| 1.1 | T |
| 1.2 | T |
| 1.3 | F |
| 1.4 | F |
| 1.5 | F |
| 1.6 | T |
| 1.7 | T |
| 1.8 | F |
| 1.9 | T |
| 1.10 | F |
| 1.11 | F |
| 1.12 | T |
| 1.13 | F |
| 1.14 | F |
| 1.15 | F |
| 1.16 | T |
| 1.17 | F |
| 1.18 | T |
| 1.19 | F |
| 1.20 | T |

1.21 Protestant

1.22 higher criticism, minister

1.23 pessimistic

1.24 *Far From the Madding Crowd*

1.25 *Jude the Obscure*, novelist

1.26 *Wessex Poems*, 1898

1.27 verse forms, common people

1.28 Theologians and preachers who have questioned the truth of Scripture

1.29 The stories add a romantic air to religion.

1.30 He agrees with Voltaire, in that, religion should be destroyed because it is useless.

1.31 The poet is trying to describe the lack of meaning in life caused by God's absence.

1.32 Their relationship is passionless and meaningless.

1.33 Without God, everything is meaningless and love is impossible.

| | |
|---|---|
| 1.34 | a |
| 1.35 | b |
| 1.36 | d |
| 1.37 | a |
| 1.38 | b |
| 1.39 | c |
| 1.40 | b |

1.41 His journey on a steamboat up the Congo

1.42 Marlow is telling his tale to a group of men from the Company on board a ship that is docked on the Thames.

1.43 He is drawing a comparison between himself and the Roman soldiers who conquered England thousands of years ago.

1.44 Marlowe says that the city makes him think of a "whited sepulchre" and the headquarters is the biggest thing in town. He goes on to underscore his impression that the Company is full of dead men by describing the streets and the buildings around it in shadowy, dark terms. The people inside the Company headquarters, especially the two women, are pictured as agents of death. The secretary is said to have white hair and skinny fingers like a dead woman.

1.45 The natives are sickly, poor, and oppressed.

1.46 He describes him as a "universal genius", the best that European idealism could produce.

1.47 It is a dark and sinister place.

1.48 So that they can eat them

1.49 The pilgrims fear that Kurtz has died.

1.50 He is implying that Kurtz is dead inside.

1.51 Kurtz "enlarged" his mind.

1.52 She is a gorgeous woman, adorned in lavish clothes and jewels.

1.53 Kurtz is utterly depraved.

1.54 The two women at the Company headquarters

1.55 "The horror. The horror."

1.56 Marlowe says that Kurtz last words were her name because it would have been too dark, too much of reality to tell her the truth.

1.57 England

1.58 journalist

1.59 First World War, German

1.60 *G. K.'s Weekly*

1.61    orthodox Christianity

1.62    appreciated

1.63    They do not allow themselves or others to think freely.

1.64    Their strict materialistic view of the world does not allow them to think freely about the possibility of the supernatural.

1.65    All religions of the earth use similar external methods of worship, devotion, and community. However, they differ greatly in their beliefs, especially on the means of salvation.

1.66    The means of dealing with the problem of sin.

1.67    He believes that the only way love for God and love for others is possible is if souls are separate.

1.68    There is no motivation to transcend or rise above your current moral state because according to pantheism everyone is on the same level. One thing is as good as another. All is relative.

1.69    the transcendence of God

1.70    Eastern civilization is based on the belief that God is strictly immanent. They have no transcendent being or state to compare their condition with and cannot conclude that things need to be changed. Therefore, the people of the east are turned inwards and blinded to the cruelty and injustice done to them.

1.71    It has insisted on the theological free will.

1.72    an active will or desire to change things

1.73    old orthodoxy

1.74    Orthodox Christianity is the only true basis of liberty, humanity, and love.

**SECTION TWO**

2.1     Dublin, Ireland

2.2     Rhymers' Club, myths, legends

2.3     Irish, William Blake, Edmund Spenser

2.4     national

2.5     Maud Gonne

2.6     realistic

2.7     mystical

2.8     Nobel Prize

2.9     It is idleness.

2.10    Like all work, the creation of poetry was subject to the fall of man and requires "much labouring."

2.11    the art of love or romance

2.12    weary-hearted

2.13    Old age is despised.

2.14    Because he does not want to grow old and be despised.

2.15    Byzantium is the place of artists and craftsmen, who are the chief communicators of spiritual truths.

2.16    So that he can be made into a thing of beauty forever.

2.17    He will not have a natural, physical body.

2.18    St. Louis, Missouri.

2.19    Harvard University

2.20    Ezra Pound

2.21    *The Love Song of J. Alfred Prufrock*

2.22    *The Wasteland*

2.23    stream of consciousness

2.24    Great Britain

2.25    *Four Quartets*

2.26    Nobel, 1948

2.27    Dante's *Inferno*

2.28    a man who anticipates telling a woman at a tea party that he loves her

2.29    They are empty and meaningless.

2.30    he is anxious about approaching the woman

2.31    his physical appearance

2.32    no

2.33    His life is full of trite acts that amount to nothing.

2.34    He fears rejection and has feelings of inadequacy.

2.35    He says it would have been impossible to say exactly what he meant.

2.36    mermaids

2.37    the sound of human voices from the tea room

2.38    When his fantasy about being courageous in love ends, he realizes that inside he is dead.

2.39    Dublin, Ireland

2.40    Fabian Society

2.41    capitalism

2.42    plays

2.43    Nobel Prize

2.44    "Life Force"

2.45    T

2.46    T

2.47    T

2.48    T

2.49    F

2.50    T

2.51    F

2.52    T

2.53    T

2.54    T

2.55    F

2.56    F

2.57    F

2.58    a

2.59    b

2.60    c

2.61    d

2.62    b

2.63    c

2.64    to form a new administration

2.65    The task of the new administration will be a difficult one.

2.66    to wage war

2.67    victory

2.68    He tells them that if they are not victorious then all that the British Empire has stood for will not survive.

2.69    There is hope for final victory.

2.70    He knows that the tide can turn unexpectedly in war, and therefore, threats should be taken as a good reason for intense vigilance and exertion.

2.71    the survival of Christian civilization

2.72    England's downfall is the key to victory.

2.73    If the Nazis win the war then the whole world will "sink into the abyss of a new Dark Age made more sinister, and perhaps more protracted, by the lights of perverted science."

2.74    Their faithful efforts will be remembered as the "finest hour" in British history.

**SECTION THREE**

3.1 home

3.2 Bloomsbury Group

3.3 women's suffrage movement

3.4 Leonard Woolf

3.5 Hogarth Press

3.6 stream of consciousness

3.7 Oliver Bacon is a middle-class merchant who seeks the society and approval of the upper class.

3.8 no

3.9 selling stolen dogs to upper class ladies

3.10 that he would be the richest jeweler in England

3.11 Bacon's mother

3.12 her love for gambling, which creates the need to sell her jewelry

3.13 his mother's voice in his head

3.14 the hope that he will remain the duchess' friend and thus gain access to her daughter, Diane

3.15 Oliver has flashbacks to when he was a boy selling stolen dogs to fashionable women because his dealings with the duchess are very similar.

3.16 fake

3.17 her "very large, very fat" body tightly fitted in pink taffeta conjures up the image of a pig

3.18 As the "daughter of hundred Earls" the duchess has the power to turn Bacon's clientele against him, ruining his much sought after approval of the upper class.

3.19 Oliver is dissatisfied with his dealings with the Duchess because he has spent his life and his fortune trying to win the favor of upper-class society but has only remained at best a middle-class merchant.

3.20 Dublin

3.21 Roman Catholic

3.22 *Dubliners*

3.23 *A Portrait of the Artist as a Young Man*

3.24 *Ulysses*

3.25 Finnegans Wake

3.26 it is a shadowy place, lacking meaning and vibrancy

3.27 winter

3.28 It makes her stand out to him against his gloomy, shadowy environment.

3.29 There is a retreat in her convent.

3.30 The boy goes to the bazaar because he wants to buy a gift for the girl.

3.31 He is infatuated with her.

3.32 Every other pursuit seems rather unimportant when compared to his crusade to win the girl's affection.

3.33 His uncle comes home late with the needed money to get buy the gift.

3.34 It is dark, empty and silent.

3.35 like a tomb

3.36 They are English.

3.37 He realizes that his romantic pursuits are meaningless and empty.

3.38 the fading significance of the church in the modern world

3.39 The boy eventually sees himself as a "creature driven and derided by vanity" because his effort to buy something for the girl resulted only in frustration and anger.

3.40 Darwinism

3.41 eyesight

3.42 *Crome Yellow*

3.43 friends

3.44 *Brave New World*

3.45 mysticism

3.46 They provoke feelings in people.

3.47 It has youth and prosperity right up until death.

3.48 as an absence

3.49 We are conditioned to believe them.

3.50 He makes sure that people are never alone and always distracted by pleasures.

3.51 They have degraded mankind.

3.52 It is properly ordered. Nobility and heroism is the symptom of political inefficiency.

3.53 belief in the existence of God

3.54 Soma makes you indifferent or numb "unpleasant" experiences, causing you behave in a kind manner toward other people. Therefore, there is no struggle to be "good."

3.55    suffering, freedom, nobility, passion, sin, goodness, and disease

3.56    C. S. Lewis

3.57    Belfast, Ireland

3.58    mythology

3.59    Oxford

3.60    Cambridge

3.61    J. R. R. Tolkien

3.62    Inklings

3.63    basic Christian beliefs

3.64    *The Screwtape Letters*

3.65    *Surprised by Joy*

3.66    The Chronicles of Narnia

3.67    acknowledging his faith and its opposition to the opinions of his friends

3.68    Few contain warnings about Worldly vanities, Choice of friends, and Value of time.

3.69    satan's demons

3.70    That he is being a witness to them, and to not associate with them would be "Puritanical."

3.71    to destroy any chances of people having spiritually healthy and happy marriages

3.72    A woman's appearance is the most important aspect of her attractiveness.

3.73    to cause him long-lasting unhappiness

3.74    that he will become increasingly ill-tempered

3.75    immoral behavior

3.76    as a pronoun of "ownership"

3.77    So that men come to understand God to be "the God on whom I have a claim for my distinguished services and whom I exploit from the pulpit the God I have done a comer in."

3.78    "Christianity And"

3.79    It is an endless source of heresy, unfaithfulness, and foolishness.

3.80    the pleasure of novelty

3.81    to distract men from real dangers

3.82    Nonsense of the intellect is used to reinforce corruption of the will.

**SELF TEST 1**

| | | | |
|---|---|---|---|
| 1.01 | literature, honor, delightful | 1.051 | epic |
| 1.02 | medieval | 1.052 | Scandinavia |
| 1.03 | Rome, Renaissance | 1.053 | heroic |
| 1.04 | intellectual, spiritual | 1.054 | Christian |
| 1.05 | Anglo-Saxons | 1.055 | worldview |
| 1.06 | Norman | 1.056 | kenning |
| 1.07 | dialect | 1.057 | salvation |
| 1.08 | Angles, Jutes | | |
| 1.09 | Paganism | | |

1.010 Christianity
1.011 heroic ideal
1.012 oral
1.013 *Beowulf*
1.014 Scops
1.015 Roman Catholicism
1.016 Scotland
1.017 Alfred
1.018 Old English
1.019 England
1.020 feudalism
1.021 French
1.022 Middle
1.023 Romance
1.024 Middle Ages
1.025 Pope
1.026 John Wycliffe
1.027 plays
1.028 Mystery
1.029 Morality
1.030 piety
1.031 England
1.032 Old English
1.033 oral-formulaic

1.034 T
1.035 F
1.036 T
1.037 F
1.038 T
1.039 T
1.040 F
1.041 T
1.042 F
1.043 T
1.044 T
1.045 F
.046 T
.047 T
.048 T
.049 F
.050 F

**For Thought and Discussion:**

Caedmon was an illiterate farmhand that was miraculously given the ability to compose religious poems and songs. After being given this gift, he was persuaded to take up the monastic life so that he might learn more of the Scriptures. Caedmon's songs sought to excite people to love religion and put away vice. However, because he could not read, his knowledge and understanding of God's Word was dependent upon the interpretations of others, namely those of the Roman Catholic faith. Therefore, Caedmon had no means by which to test his beliefs and the beliefs of others.

Guide your student in a discussion of the importance of individual study of the Scriptures. Help your student understand that every Christian needs to follow the Bereans example in Acts 17:11. We need to "receive the word with all readiness" and search the Scriptures daily to find out whether the teachings that we have heard are actually biblical. 2 Timothy 3:16, 17 emphasizes the fact that the Scriptures are "God-breathed," and therefore, the final authority in faith and life. It is God's direct revelation to man. As one writer has noted, "[The Scriptures] are clear, so that a person without special preparation can understand what God requires without the intervention of an official interpreter."

**SELF TEST 2**

2.01   John Wycliffe
2.02   Old English
2.03   human
2.04   middle
2.05   Parliament
2.06   characters
2.07   Italian
2.08   English
2.09   four
2.010  Middle Ages

2.011  T
2.012  F
2.013  T
2.014  T
2.015  T
2.016  T
2.017  T
2.018  F
2.019  F
2.020  T
2.021  F
2.022  F
2.023  T
2.024  T
2.025  T
2.026  T
2.027  T
2.028  T
2.029  F
2.030  T
2.031  F
2.032  F
2.033  F
2.034  T
2.035  F
2.036  T
2.037  T
2.038  T
2.039  F
2.040  T
2.041  T
2.042  T
2.043  T
2.044  T
2.045  F
2.046  T

2.047  Rome
2.048  Anglo-Saxons
2.049  Norman

2.050  Middle
2.051  heroic
2.052  church, reform
2.053  society
2.054  1372
2.055  William Langland
2.056  commoners
2.057  neighbor
2.058  visions, allegory

**For Thought and Discussion:**

The Pardoner is a figure of the corruption and hypocrisy of the Roman Catholic Church. He earns his living by selling pardons and indulgences to ignorant people. (During the Middle Ages, officials of the Roman Catholic Church sold pardons and indulgences for the forgiveness of sins.) Though admittedly guilty of the sins which he preaches against, the Pardoner is boldly unrepentant. His favorite text is "Love of money is the root of all evil." Yet, his whole purpose in preaching is to induce people to buy pardons from him. Chaucer's description of the Pardoner emphasizes his perversity. His feminine features and voice imply that he practices some form of sexual immorality.

Guide your student in a discussion of the Pardoner in light of 2 Timothy 3:1-5. Help them to understand that Christians must turn away from people that give an "appearance of godliness but [deny] its power." Throughout Scripture, God's people are warned against false teachers. Men like the Pardoner exist today as they did at the time of the apostles. Like the Pardoner, they use religion to gain wealth, prestige and fame. They have no sincere love for God's Word or His people. They are "lovers of themselves, lovers of money, boasters proud, blasphemers, disobedient to parents unthankful, unholy, unloving, unforgiving, slanders, without self-control, brutal, despisers of good traitors, headstrong, haughty, lovers of pleasure rather than lovers of God." Jesus described false teachers as wolves in sheep's clothing. The only way to guard against the influence of false teachers is to search the Scriptures daily to see if what they teach is true (cf. Acts 17:11). Teachers like the Pardoner have no power over individuals that have a thorough knowledge of God's Word.

**SELF TEST 3**

| | |
|---|---|
| 3.01 | Old English |
| 3.02 | John Wycliffe |
| 3.03 | human |
| 3.04 | Italian |
| 3.05 | unfinished |
| 3.06 | morality |
| 3.07 | Mystery |
| 3.08 | Moralities |
| 3.09 | Moralities |
| 3.010 | Roman Catholic |
| 3.011 | good deeds |

| | |
|---|---|
| 3.012 | T |
| 3.013 | F |
| 3.014 | T |
| 3.015 | T |
| 3.016 | T |
| 3.017 | T |
| 3.018 | T |
| 3.019 | T |
| 3.020 | F |
| 3.021 | T |
| 3.022 | T |
| 3.023 | T |
| 3.024 | F |
| 3.025 | F |
| 3.026 | F |

| | |
|---|---|
| 3.027 | Rome |
| 3.028 | Anglo-Saxon |
| 3.029 | Norman |
| 3.030 | Middle |
| 3.031 | heroic |
| 3.032 | church |
| 3.033 | neighbor |
| 3.034 | Yorkist |
| 3.035 | *Le Morte d' Arthur* |
| 3.036 | King Arthur |

| | |
|---|---|
| 3.037 | F |
| 3.038 | T |
| 3.039 | T |
| 3.040 | F |
| 3.041 | F |
| 3.042 | F |
| 3.043 | T |
| 3.044 | T |
| 3.045 | T |
| 3.046 | F |
| 3.047 | T |
| 3.048 | F |

| | |
|---|---|
| 3.049 | F |
| 3.050 | F |
| 3.051 | F |
| 3.052 | F |
| 3.053 | T |

**For Thought and Discussion:**

*Everyman* is a morality play based on the beliefs of Medieval Roman Catholicism. Morality plays dramatize the moral struggle of the common man through the use of allegory. In the play, the character Everyman is told that he must meet death. He, at first, tries to avoid the confrontation but is unsuccessful. Realizing that the meeting is inevitable, he tries to bring his friends and earthly goods with him. However, they quickly leave him. Everyman is only able to bring Good Deeds and Knowledge with him on his journey to meet Death. As Everyman begins to descend into the grave, Knowledge stands over him. Good Deeds follows him.

Guide your student in a discussion on the play's assertion that good deeds help us to be accepted by God. In light of Ephesians 2:8-9, help the student to understand that good works do not make us more acceptable to God. Rather, good deeds are the result of God's gracious transformation of the Christian (Ezekiel 36:25-27; Ephesians 1:4, 2:10; Philippians 2:13). The Bible asserts that salvation is a gift of God. The only thing that we contribute to our salvation, as one writer has put it, is our sin. Our righteousness or good deeds are so tainted with sinful motives that they are like filthy rags in the presence of God (Isaiah 64:6). Contrary to the teachings of Medieval Roman Catholicism, Scripture states that faith in Christ's good deeds is the only thing that will "help us" before God (Romans 1:17; 2 Corinthians 5:21; Philippians 3:9).

**SELF TEST 1**

| | |
|---|---|
| 1.01 | Reformation |
| 1.02 | Word of God |
| 1.03 | Renaissance |
| 1.04 | church |
| 1.05 | Scripture |
| 1.06 | Reformation |
| 1.07 | William Tyndale |
| 1.08 | Catholic |
| 1.09 | Edward VI |
| 1.010 | Protestants |
| 1.011 | Anglican |
| 1.012 | independent, nations |
| 1.013 | English |
| 1.014 | sonnet |
| 1.015 | fourteen |
| 1.016 | English |
| 1.017 | pastoral |
| 1.018 | Seneca, classical, horror |
| 1.019 | English history |
| 1.020 | tragedy, destruction |
| 1.021 | oval |
| 1.022 | Elizabethan |
| 1.023 | Lord Chancellor |
| 1.024 | *Utopia* |
| 1.025 | reason |
| 1.026 | no place |
| 1.027 | treason, Henry VIII |
| 1.028 | Scripture |
| 1.029 | Roger Ascham |
| 1.030 | *The Schoolmaster* |
| 1.031 | Oxford, Greek, faith |
| 1.032 | England |
| 1.033 | historical, evangelicalism, Biblical |

| | |
|---|---|
| 1.034 | F |
| 1.035 | T |
| 1.036 | T |
| 1.037 | T |
| 1.038 | T |
| 1.039 | F |
| 1.040 | F |
| 1.041 | T |
| 1.042 | T |
| 1.043 | T |
| 1.044 | T |
| 1.045 | T |
| 1.046 | T |
| 1.047 | T |
| 1.048 | F |
| 1.049 | T |
| 1.050 | T |

**For Thought and Discussion:**

The Renaissance was a movement that placed great value on the wisdom of the ancient Greeks and Romans. It emphasized the concept that human reason was untainted. Its proper use could lead one to truth. As a student of the Renaissance, Sir Thomas More recognized the capabilities of human reason. However, he also recognized its limitations. Many scholars view his masterpiece, *Utopia*, as a work of satire. The word utopia in Greek means "no place." It is probable that More is saying that a world based solely upon human wisdom is "no place" to be found. Considering the sinfulness of man, its existence is impossible. However, there are others in more modern times that have interpreted Utopia to be an outline for a society devoid of greed, crime, pride and poverty. In the fictional Utopian Republic, gold and silver are scorned. All people work for the good of the community. No one is poor. No one starves. Properly run government institutions are the cause of society's happiness and success.

Guide your student in a discussion on the possibility of the existence of a perfect world based upon human wisdom. In light of 1 Corinthians 2:6-15, help your student to understand that those that follow the wisdom of the world will come to nothing. Their societies, no matter how perfect they may appear at first, will eventually break down.

A primary example is the history of the Union of Soviet Socialist Republics. The U.S.S.R. was based upon the economic theories of Karl Marx, the father communism. As in *Utopia*, Marx envisioned a perfect society where no one was poor and everyone worked for the good of the community. To many, Marx's communistic principles seemed the idea solution to problems in society fueled by greed and pride. However Marx's theories were based upon human reason, or rather, worldly wisdom. He called religion the opiate of the masses, scorning the "spiritual wisdom" of Christianity. Time has both revealed Marx's foolishness and the truth of Scripture. 1 Corinthians 3:18-21 states that "If anyone among you seems to be wise in this age, let him become a fool that he may become wise. For the wisdom of this world is foolishness with God. For it is written, *'He catches the wise in their own craftiness'*; and again, *'The LORD knows the thoughts of the wise, that they are futile.'* Therefore let no one boast in men."

In this life, sin has made the existence of a perfect society impossible. However, when Christ returns establish the New Jerusalem, the redeemed shall live in perfect communion with God and with each other "There shall be no more death, nor sorrow, nor crying. There shall be no more pain, for the former thing [will] have passed away" (Revelation 21:4).

## SELF TEST 2

| | |
|---|---|
| 2.01 | Utopia |
| 2.02 | Scripture |
| 2.03 | historical |
| 2.04 | Queen Elizabeth |
| 2.05 | England |
| 2.06 | conceit |
| 2.07 | Petrarchian, fourteen, octave |
| 2.08 | question, sestet |
| 2.09 | rhyme scheme |
| 2.010 | three |
| 2.011 | English |
| 2.012 | Cambridge |
| 2.013 | pastoral |
| 2.014 | Chaucer |
| 2.015 | Sir Walter Raleigh |
| 2.016 | "Amoretti" |
| 2.017 | archaic, chivalry |
| 2.018 | Sir Philip Sidney |
| 2.019 | divine |

| | |
|---|---|
| 2.020 | F |
| 2.021 | T |
| 2.022 | T |
| 2.023 | T |
| 2.024 | T |
| 2.025 | F |
| 2.026 | T |
| 2.027 | F |
| 2.028 | F |
| 2.029 | T |
| 2.030 | T |
| 2.031 | F |
| 2.032 | F |
| 2.033 | T |
| 2.034 | T |
| 2.035 | T |
| 2.036 | F |
| 2.037 | T |
| 2.038 | T |
| .039 | T |
| .040 | T |
| .041 | F |
| .042 | T |
| .043 | T |
| .044 | F |

| | |
|---|---|
| 045 | Renaissance |
| 046 | Scripture |
| 047 | sonnet |
| 048 | Elizabethan |
| 049 | Catholic |
| 050 | pastoral romance |
| 051 | sonnet sequence |

| | |
|---|---|
| 2.052 | *The Defense of Posey* |
| 2.053 | courtier |
| 2.054 | wanting |
| 2.055 | mischief |
| 2.056 | snake |

## For Thought and Discussion:

Edmund Spenser was a Christian that often wrote in a highly allegorical language. The section of *The Faerie Queen* included in the student's text describes the Red Cross Knight's encounter with the monster Error when he strays from the sure path and becomes lost in the darkness of the woods. The Red Cross Knight represents the Christian as he struggles to resist temptation and live a life that is pleasing to His Lord. He is accompanied by a lovely lady who is represents both truth and true religion, as opposed to the Catholic religion. Her white donkey is symbolic of the pure church, which carries truth to the corners of the world. The monster Error is the personification of evil. Like the serpent in the garden, Error strives against God by perverting the truth and ensnaring His children in sin.

Guide your student in a discussion of the similarities between Spenser's story and Genesis 3, Matthew 21:1-11, Ephesians 6, and Revelation 16:13. Help your student to understand how the characters illustrate. Biblical truth. Genesis 3 describes the temptation and fall of man in the garden. In *The Faerie Queen*, Spenser combines the two tempting figures in the Genesis account, the serpent and the woman, into one being. The monster Error is describes as half-serpent and half-woman.

Matthew 21:1-11 describes Jesus' triumphal entry into Jerusalem on a donkey. The lovely lady rides upon a donkey, identifying her with Jesus, the Way, the Truth and the Life. Spenser's donkey is described as white, therefore, pure and undefiled like the donkey that Jesus rode, which was a colt and had not been ridden by anyone.

Ephesians 6 encourages the Christian to protect himself from the schemes of the devil by putting on the whole armor of God. The Red Cross Knight is dressed in armor from head to toe. Upon his breastplate and his shield is a red cross, in remembrance of his "dying Lord." When the Knight begins to succumb to the powers of Error, the lovely lady exhorts him to "add faith to his force" or rather, as Ephesians 6:10 states, "be strong in the Lord and in the power of His might," in order that he might escape.

Revelation 16:13 describes in allegorical terms Satan's last great effort to ensnare mankind. As Matthew Henry has observed, the three unclean spirits represent respectively, the instruments of "hell, the secular power of antichrist, and the ecclesiastical power" to cause havoc with "hellish malice, with worldly policy, and with religious falsehood and deceit." Similar to this passage, Spenser describes the vomit of the monster Error to be full of heretical "bookes and papers" and "loathly frogs and toades."

**SELF TEST 3**

| | |
|---|---|
| 3.01 | Scripture |
| 3.02 | Renaissance |
| 3.03 | Elizabethan |
| 3.04 | courtier |
| 3.05 | sonnet sequence |
| 3.06 | poet |
| 3.07 | Queen Elizabeth's |
| 3.08 | King James |
| 3.09 | Stratford-on-Avon |
| 3.010 | Anne Hathaway |
| 3.011 | narrative poem |
| 3.012 | First Folio, 1623 |
| 3.013 | tragedies |
| 3.014 | Reformation |
| 3.015 | translating the Bible |
| 3.016 | English |
| 3.017 | Geneva Bible |
| 3.018 | Latin Vulgate |
| 3.019 | King James Version, people |

| | |
|---|---|
| 3.020 | F |
| 3.021 | T |
| 3.022 | T |
| 3.023 | T |
| 3.024 | T |
| 3.025 | F |
| 3.026 | T |
| 3.027 | T |
| 3.028 | F |
| 3.029 | T |
| 3.030 | T |
| 3.031 | F |
| 3.032 | F |
| 3.033 | F |
| 3.034 | F |
| 3.035 | T |
| 3.036 | F |
| 3.037 | T |
| 3.038 | T |
| 3.039 | T |
| 3.040 | F |
| 3.041 | T |
| 3.042 | F |
| 3.043 | F |
| 3.044 | T |

| | |
|---|---|
| .045 | historical |
| .046 | *Utopia* |
| .047 | Scripture, learning |
| .048 | England |
| 049 | conceit |
| 050 | archaic, chivalry |
| 051 | divine |

| | |
|---|---|
| 3.052 | ever-fixed |
| 3.053 | roses |
| 3.054 | music |
| 3.055 | rare |
| 3.056 | plagued, humbled |
| 3.057 | leper |
| 3.058 | Geneva |

**For Thought and Discussion:**

*The Taming of the Shrew* is a comedy. By definition, it begins with some type of disturbance then progresses to affliction and ends in restoration. Though a love story filled with humor and wit, the possibility of tragedy is real. Throughout the play you are kept guessing as to how the play will end.

Petruchio and Katherine ("Kate") are the central characters in *The Taming of the Shrew*. Petruchio is desirous of a wife. Katherine, the eldest daughter of the wealthy Baptista, becomes the object of his "love." But Katherine is not a gentle, kind person. Like an unloved and undisciplined child, she throws fits and lashes out with cruel words. In the city of Padua, she has earned for herself a reputation as a Shrew. (A shrew is a tiny mouse-like creature, possessing a violent manner.) Upon seeing Katherine's behavior, Petruchio determines to change her by "education." He is a man that loves a challenge. But, Petruchio's friends warn him that Kate is a "fiend of hell" and any attempt to make her his gentle, obedient bride will only bring him to a tragic end. Nevertheless, Petruchio marries Kate. To everyone's surprise, he arrives late to the ceremony and is dressed wildly. On their wedding night, Petruchio behaves rudely toward his new bride. He does not allow her to eat or sleep. Petruchio's behavior is an attempt to make Kate see how ridiculous it is to be a shrew. While on the trip back to her father's house, Kate finally realizes the goodness in submitting to a man that cares for her. At the end of the play, Petruchio proves to his fellows that he has through love transformed the Shrew into a gentle, obedient wife.

In light of Ephesians 5:22-33, guide your student in a discussion of the resemblance of Petruchio and Katherine to Christ and the church. Help your student to understand how Petruchio, as a husband, sanctifies and cleanses Katherine.

Peter Leithart has observed in his commentary on the play that "Kate's progress is from bestial savagery and ferocity to tame and gentle womanhood. Petruchio represents the power of civilization and religion, which employs authority and even force to

shape a depraved humanity. Petruchio, like Christ, is preparing a savage child of hell to become Queen at his right hand." Kate's change is the product of Petruchio's love for her. It was not was not she that choose him, but he that choose her. As Christ gave Himself for the church, that He might make it holy, so Petruchio committed himself to Kate, enduring her cruel treatment of him, in order that she might be changed. Like Christ, Petruchio affects these changes by transforming her whole outlook on life; he changes her from the inside out. As one writer has noted, his word, his perception of reality is the key to this transformation. Petruchio sanctifies or sets her apart as his own by giving her a different name. This also signifies a change in identity. "Kate," not Katherine the shrew, is Petruchio's beloved. Petruchio cleanses Kate of her disobedient way by insisting that she follow his leadership. When he calls the sun the moon and a man a maiden, Kate must submit and acknowledge that he is right (Act 4, Scene 5), though she thinks otherwise. Kate is sanctified and cleansed from her former way of life when she submits to her husband's will in all things. Likewise the Christian is sanctified and cleansed when God loving shapes our hearts to live in humble obedience to His Word. Kate's speech at the end of Act 5 pictures marriage as a loving relationship in which the husband provides and protects and the wife helps and obeys. Her reasons for a wife's submission seem to be taken directly from Ephesians 5:22-33. The influence of Reformed Christianity upon Shakespeare and more generally Elizabethan culture is quite obvious in this play.

## SELF TEST 1

1.01    F
1.02    T
1.03    F
1.04    T
1.05    T
1.06    T
1.07    T
1.08    T
1.09    F
1.010   T
1.011   T
1.012   T

1.013   Royal Chaplain
1.014   metaphysical
1.015   Jack Donne, Rev. John Donne
1.016   Puritan
1.017   Westminster School
1.018   playwright
1.019   William Shakespeare
1.020   Cavalier
1.021   classical

1.022   b
1.023   a
1.024   c
1.025   b
1.026   c
1.027   c
1.028   a
1.029   c
1.030   a
1.031   c
1.032   b
1.033   b
1.034   c
1.035   b

.036    minister
.037    Anglican
.038    poetry
.039    metaphysical

**For Thought and Discussion:**

Ben Jonson and John Donne represent two schools of poetic style during the Stuart period. Ben Jonson is considered the father of the Cavalier School of poets. The Cavalier poets were associated with the court of Charles I. Written in a lighthearted, polished, and witty manner, their poems sought to uphold traditional attitudes towards the throne, war, and romantic love, in society. Jonson understood the role of poet to be a public one. As in ancient times, it was his duty to guide and correct the people on matters that affected society.

As the first metaphysical poet, John Donne stands in direct contrast to Ben Jonson. Donne rejected the conventions of Elizabethan or traditional love poetry and instead wrote in an allusive, complex and often obscure manner. His "metaphysical wit" tended to focus on abstract concepts. Unlike the Jonson's Cavalier school, Donne wrote about the psychological effects of love or religion rather than the physical effects.

Guide your student in a discussion of the two schools of poetry. Help him to articulate *fully* the reasons behind his preference for one or the other style. Read the selected poems over again to help him draw a well thought out conclusion.

**SELF TEST 2**

| | |
|---|---|
| 2.01 | F |
| 2.02 | T |
| 2.03 | T |
| 2.04 | T |
| 2.05 | F |
| 2.06 | T |
| 2.07 | T |
| 2.08 | T |
| | |
| 2.09 | poetry |
| 2.010 | metaphysical |
| 2.011 | Renaissance |
| 2.012 | Parliamentary supporter |
| 2.013 | Independent |
| 2.014 | Oliver Cromwell |
| 2.015 | *Paradise Lost* |
| | |
| 2.016 | a |
| 2.017 | c |
| 2.018 | a |
| 2.019 | b |
| 2.020 | d |
| 2.021 | a |
| 2.022 | b |
| 2.023 | a |
| 2.024 | d |
| 2.025 | b |
| 2.026 | b |
| 2.027 | b |
| 2.028 | a |
| 2.029 | d |
| 2.030 | d |
| 2.031 | c |
| 2.032 | b |
| | |
| 2.033 | metaphysical |
| 2.034 | Cavalier |
| 2.035 | classical |
| 2.036 | Laud, Word of God |
| 2.037 | Rump, Oliver Cromwell |
| 2.038 | physical |
| 2.039 | scientific |
| 2.040 | James I |

**For Thought and Discussion:**

*Paradise Lost* was written by John Milton in an attempt to "justify the ways of God to men." Centered on Adam and Eve's freedom to choose between good or evil, the work illustrates vividly the biblical answers to the existence of evil, the fall of man, and the consequences that have ensued. Paralleling passages in Genesis 1-3, Job, the Epistles, and Revelation, Milton takes up his "great argument" in defense of God's sovereignty and goodness, laying the fault of the world's sin and corruption at the feet of man.

The excerpts from *Paradise Lost* that are included in the text cover God's foretelling of mankind's fall, the Son's free offer of Himself for man's sin, Satan's scheme to corrupt mankind, the deception of Eve by the Serpent, Adam's decision to perish with his wife, and the immediate effects of their sin. Milton characterizes God as the gracious and sovereign Creator of Adam and Eve. The Son is pictured as a willing sacrifice, worthy of the highest adoration. Satan is the personification of evil, who seeks to corrupt all that is good. Eve is pictured as the "weaker vessel," in need of guidance and protection. Adam is the wise husband who agrees to eat the fruit out of love for his wife. It must be noted at this point, that Milton attributes motivations for Adam's eating of the fruit that are found nowhere in Scripture. His conclusion that Adam fell because he did not want his wife to perish alone is more in line with medieval concepts of the evil of women and the goodness of men than with the truth of Scripture. As head of his wife and the chosen representative of mankind, Adam is ultimately responsible for sin entering the world (Romans 5:12-19).

Guide your student in a discussion of the causes and the consequences of man's disobedience described by Milton. Help him to understand that the consequences of sin is death, both physically and spiritually. The immediate ramifications of Adam and Eve's sin was strife, physical suffering and pain (Genesis 3:14-19). In *Paradise Lost*, Milton pictures the immediate consequences of the fall to be discord. Adam and Eve blame each other, hoping to remove their own guilt and shame. Though it promises happiness, sin only results in long-lasting strife, suffering and pain. Galatians 6:7-8 states, "Do not be deceived, God is not mocked; for whatever a man sows, that he will also reap. For he who sows to his flesh will of the flesh reap corruption, but he who sows to the Spirit will of the Spirit reap everlasting life." Mankind's only means of joy and peace may be found in loving obedience to God wrought by the work of the Holy Spirit (cf. Ezekiel 36:24-30, John 15:5-11).

**SELF TEST 3**

| | |
|---|---|
| 3.01 | F |
| 3.02 | T |
| 3.03 | F |
| 3.04 | T |
| 3.05 | F |
| 3.06 | T |
| 3.07 | T |
| 3.08 | F |
| 3.09 | T |
| 3.010 | T |
| 3.011 | T |
| 3.012 | T |
| 3.013 | T |
| 3.014 | T |
| 3.015 | F |
| 3.016 | T |
| 3.017 | F |
| 3.018 | T |
| 3.019 | F |

| | |
|---|---|
| 3.020 | occasional |
| 3.021 | Neoclassical |
| 3.022 | prose |
| 3.023 | Enlightenment |
| 3.024 | Tory |
| 3.025 | Irish |
| 3.026 | hymns, hymnody |
| 3.027 | Neoclassical |
| 3.028 | Reformed |
| 3.029 | metaphysical |
| 3.030 | *Paradise Lost* |
| 3.031 | physical |
| 3.032 | Oliver Cromwell |
| 3.033 | allegories |
| 3.034 | tinker |
| 3.035 | preaching |
| 3.036 | Bible |
| 3.037 | Greek, Roman |
| 3.038 | satires |
| 3.039 | man |
| 3.040 | heroic |

| | |
|---|---|
| 3.041 | a |
| 3.042 | c |
| 3.043 | b |
| 3.044 | d |
| 3.045 | c |
| 3.046 | b |
| 3.047 | a |
| 3.048 | c |
| 3.049 | b |
| 3.050 | a |
| 3.051 | b |

| | |
|---|---|
| 3.052 | c |
| 3.053 | b |
| 3.054 | a |
| 3.055 | b |
| 3.056 | b |
| 3.057 | a |
| 3.058 | c |

**For Thought and Discussion:**

Initially, John Bunyan hesitated to have *Pilgrim's Progress* published. He feared that fiction was not a proper genre to convey the pathway to godliness. However, Bunyan finally concluded that *Pilgrim's Progress* is a collection of parables not unlike those found in the Bible and used by Jesus to teach divine truth. In "The Author's Apology for his Book," Bunyan wrote:

> Solidity, indeed, becomes the pen
> Of him that writeth things divine to men;
> But must I needs want solidness, because
> By metaphors I speak? Were not God's laws,
> His gospel laws, in olden time held forth
> By types, shadows, and metaphors? Yet loth
> Will any sober man be to find fault
> With them, lest he be to found for to assault
> The highest wisdom. No, he rather stoops,
> And seeks to find out what by pins and loops,
> By calves and sheep, by heifers and by rams,
> By birds and herbs, and by the blood of lambs,
> God speaketh to him. And happy is he
> That finds the light and grace that in them be...
>
> My dark and cloudy words they do but hold
> The truth, as cabinets enclose the gold.
>   The prophets used much by metaphors
> To set forth truth; yea, whoso considers
> Christ, His apostles too, shall plainly see
> That truths to this day in such mantles be.
>   Am I afraid to say that holy writ,
> Which for its style and phrase puts down all wit,
> Is everywhere so full of all these things—
> Dark figures, allegories? Yet there springs
> From that same book that lustre, and those rays
> Of light, that turns our darkest nights to days...

Guide your student in a discussion of Bunyan's use of commonplace experiences and events to convey deeply meaningful spiritual truths. Help him to understand that Bunyan's use of allegory in *Pilgrim's Progress* is similar to Christ's use of parables. To compare, read the parables of Jesus found in Luke 13:6:-9, 18-30, 15:1-32. Note that Christ used commonplace experiences to convey spiritual truths. In comparing Christ's use of parables with Bunyan's, help your

student to understand that *Pilgrim's Progress* effectively and powerfully illustrates truths about the Christian life. Do this by asking your student to explain which events in Christian's journey were most meaningful to him and why. You might want to also ask him about particular events in the story. Here are some suggestions for discussion: What Biblical significance is there behind Evangelist's advice to Christian to go and knock on the wicket gate? What is the underlying message behind Christian's difficulty in the Slough of Despond? What does the burden that Christian bears represent? What is significant about the names of the men that Mr. Worldly Wiseman tells Christian to go speak to in order to find relief from his burden? What happens to Christian's burden when he comes to the Cross? What kind of people live in Vanity Fair? Why do these people persecute Faithful? Why must Christian pass through the deep river before reaching the gate to the Heavenly City? What is Ignorance ignorant of, and why is he refused entrance to Heaven?

**SELF TEST 1**

1.01    T
1.02    F
1.03    F
1.04    F
1.05    F
1.06    T
1.07    T
1.08    F
1.09    T
1.010   F

1.011   mysticism
1.012   symbolically
1.013   books
1.014   historical
1.015   legal official
1.016   poems

1.017   a
1.018   b
1.019   c
1.020   b
1.021   c
1.022   a
1.023   c
1.024   a
1.025   d
1.026   b
1.027   c
1.028   b
1.029   b
1.030   b
1.031   d
1.032   c

1.033   transcendental
1.034   *Lyrical Ballads*
1.035   mystical, idealism
1.036   *Biographia Literaria*, literary criticism
1.037   pleasure
1.038   Lake District
1.039   *Poems in Two Volumes*
1.040   Poet Laureate
1.041   *The Prelude*

**For Thought and Discussion:**

Samuel Taylor Coleridge's poem, *The Rime of the Ancient Mariner*, is a tale of a sailor who kills a friendly albatross for no reason. The sailor, now old, insists on telling his story to a passer-by who is enroute to a wedding. The sailor tells him circumstances and the results of his senseless act. While out at sea, the sailor spies an albatross flying overhead. Despite the fact that the albatross is an omen of good will, he shoots it with his crossbow. Not too long after the sailor's actions the wind ceases to blow. The ship's crew draw the conclusion that the albatross' unnecessary death at the hands of one of their own is the reason for their peril. As a symbol of shame, the crew makes the sailor wear the dead albatross around his neck. Eventually, the crew members die of lack of water. The sailor is left alive to see the results of his sin. When he takes pleasure in the sight of some eels swimming in the sea and blesses them, it is then that the albatross falls from his neck and he is able to pray. The rain comes and he is refreshed. The ship and its crew then begin to move mysteriously, inspirited by some angelic power. When the ship returns to his native country, the sailor is greeted by a hermit, whom he looks as a holy man to absolve his soul and "wash away the albatross' blood" (lines 512-513). As a means of penance, the sailor is bound to tell his "ghastly tale." For if he does not, the "agony returns" and his "heart within [him] burns" (lines 583-585). The moral of Coleridge's tale is that there are great spiritual blessings for those who love God's creation.

Conceived with the help of William Wordsworth, the poem contains both transcendental and Christian elements. The transcendental belief in the journey from disunity to unity is joined with the Christian steps toward restoration: sin, guilt, and repentance. However, because no mention is made of Christ's effective work on the cross, the poem cannot be read as a testimony to the Christian faith. Coleridge is acknowledging, if anything, the temporary emotional benefits of confession. The lasting spiritual need for repentance and faith in Christ is not affirmed.

Guide your student in a discussion of Coleridge's concept of sin and his answers to the problem of guilt in reference to Psalm 51. Help him to understand that Coleridge's concepts of sin and forgiveness are not biblical. He does not see sin as an act of rebellion against God Who alone is Holy (Psalm 51:4). Rather, Coleridge understands sin to be any violation against Nature. Hatred for God's creatures results in disunity, and therefore leads to pain and suffering.

Peace and unity are achieved when love is felt for God's creatures and then acted upon. While this is true to some extent, sin does cause division and disunity among God's created order. However, Coleridge did not understand the biblical definition of sin, nor did he understand its dire consequences. Sin is usually defined as a violation or lack of conformity to God's law (See I John 3:4) and is a damnable act. . Sin not only separates us from other people but from God Himself. The Bible says that we were conceived in sin (Psalm 51:5). Therefore, all humans are worthy of condemnation (cf. Romans 3:10-18). Forgiveness is found not in doing pentenance, or being good. For Scripture says, "Therefore by the deeds of the law no flesh will be justified in His sight, for by the law is the knowledge of sin" (Romans 3:20). On the contrary, the burden of guilt is removed when we acknowledge our sin to God and He washes away our iniquity (Psalm 51:1-4). Unlike the ancient Mariner, the Christian does not have to live in agony because of his past sins but may rejoice because "He made Him who knew no sin to be sin for us, that we might become the righteousness of God in Him" (2 Corinthians 5:21).

**SELF TEST 2**

2.01    *Lyrical Ballads*
2.02    Enlightenment
2.03    poems
2.04    William Blake's
2.05    spontaneous
2.06    *The Rime of the Ancient Mariner*

2.07    b
2.08    a
2.09    d
2.010   b
2.011   c
2.012   a
2.013   c
2.014   d
2.015   c

2.016   T
2.017   F
2.018   F
2.019   F
2.020   T
2.021   F
2.022   T
2.023   T
2.024   T
2.025   T
2.026   T
2.027   T
2.028   F

2.029   *Childe Harold's Pilgrimage*
2.030   England
2.031   *Don Juan*
2.032   relativity
2.033   Mary Godwin
2.034   1818, Italy
2.035   Pisan, "Ode to the West Wind"
2.036   imagination
2.037   1819
2.038   *Lamia, Isabella, The Eve of St. Agnes, and Other Poems*
2.039   tuberculosis
2.040   art

**For Thought and Discussion:**

Unlike his Romantic contemporaries, John Keats did not envision a golden age of man here on earth. His physical sufferings and poverty probably made this notion seem too fantastical for belief. Instead, Keats imagined a higher existence for man where the pain and distress of our earthly existence would be no more. Although Keats understanding of life after death might sound similar to the Christian hope for heaven, his beliefs are rooted in transcendental mysticism. Keats rejected the guidance of Scripture and instead held an exalted view of art. Keats believed that art alone could elevate one's senses to the spiritual realm. In Keats's understanding of reality, truth is relative to one's interpretation of what is beautiful. He saw truth and beauty as two inseparable parts. In *"Ode to a Grecian Urn"* he put it this way, "Beauty is truth, truth beauty,—that is all/Ye know on earth, and all ye need to know." Christians do not necessarily disagree with the ultimate reality of this conclusion. (That which is truly beautiful is true, and that which is true is beautiful because God is the Author of Truth, and nothing but goodness and light resides in Him.) However, Christians differ greatly with Keats on what is the standard of truth. Keats interpreted the standard of truth to be the heart of man, which is ever-changing and clouded by sin. Christians, on the other hand, understand the standard of truth to be the holy and immutable Word of God.

Guide your student in a discussion of Keats's elevated view of art in reference to Colossians 1:17 and Revelation 1:8. Help him to understand that the ultimate standard of truth and goodness is God's Word. All man-made standards are subject to change because the heart of man is ever-changing and his knowledge is limited. God, however, is changeless. He is infinite in wisdom and knowledge. Colossians 1:17 states, "And He is before all things, and in Him all things consist." God is the Author of beauty and truth. Things exist and hold together because He exists and wills them to be so. Revelation 1:8 states, "I am the Alpha and the Omega, the Beginning and the End," says the Lord, "who is and who was and who is to come, the Almighty." As the Creator and Sustainer of the Universe, He is the true measure of goodness. His Word, therefore, determines that which is true and conclusively that which is beautiful. With this in mind, it could be said that true beauty is in the eye of God rather than "in the eye of the beholder."

**SELF TEST 3**

| | |
|---|---|
| 3.01 | F |
| 3.02 | T |
| 3.03 | T |
| 3.04 | T |
| 3.05 | T |
| 3.06 | T |
| 3.07 | T |
| 3.08 | T |
| 3.09 | F |
| 3.010 | F |
| 3.011 | T |
| 3.012 | F |
| 3.013 | F |
| 3.014 | F |

| | |
|---|---|
| 3.015 | *Sartor Resartus* |
| 3.016 | strong leaders |
| 3.017 | "Sage of Chelsea" |
| 3.018 | *Scenes from Clerical Life* |
| 3.019 | evolution |

| | |
|---|---|
| 3.020 | a |
| 3.021 | c |
| 3.022 | b |
| 3.023 | a |
| 3.024 | b |
| 3.025 | a |
| 3.026 | a |
| 3.027 | b |
| 3.028 | a |
| 3.029 | a |
| 3.030 | b |
| 3.031 | d |
| 3.032 | c |
| 3.033 | d |
| 3.034 | c |
| 3.035 | a |

| | |
|---|---|
| 3.036 | F |
| 3.037 | T |
| 3.038 | T |
| 3.039 | T |
| 3.040 | F |
| 3.041 | F |

| | |
|---|---|
| 3.042 | factory, unpaid debts |
| 3.043 | *The Pickwick Papers* |
| 3.044 | editor |
| 3.045 | public readings of his works |
| 3.046 | Arthur Hallam, ten |
| 3.047 | *In Memoriam*, elegy |
| 3.048 | Tennyson |
| 3.049 | symbolic logic |
| 3.050 | The three Liddell daughters |

| | |
|---|---|
| 3.051 | relativity |
| 3.052 | art |
| 3.053 | imagination |
| 3.054 | Enlightenment |
| 3.055 | *The Rime of the Ancient Mariner* |
| 3.056 | Elizabeth Barrett |
| 3.057 | *The Ring and the Book* |
| 3.058 | Romantics |
| 3.059 | Aesthetic |
| 3.060 | *The Importance of Being Earnest.* |

**For Thought and Discussion:**

As the son of a Calvinistic Presbyterian, Thomas Carlyle aspired to be a minister. However, he soon abandoned his pursuits when he became skeptical of Christianity while studying the works of Enlightenment writers. He continued to preach, though, using his writings to broadcast his thoughts on religion and society. Carlyle's work, *Sartor Resartus*, proclaims with much vigor the basis for his rejection of orthodox Christianity. The title actually means "the tailor retailored." It refers to the "clothes philosophy" that was then popular among skeptics. Carlyle concluded that the "Hebrew Old Clothes" of traditional Christianity were worn out. Man needed to clothe himself in a new philosophy. Frustrated by the authority of Scripture and the guidance of reason, Carlyle pointed to man's heart as the fount of truth. This exaltation of man-made religious experience was of particular importance. Not willing to totally reject the idea of a personal God, Carlyle offered a new faith in which the citizen of secular society could feel a sense of religious awe yet not have to bow to the doctrines of any particular sect. Carlyle did not attack any particular doctrine of Christianity but rather criticized its followers. In *Sartor Resartus*, he describes Christianity as the "Worship of Sorrow" and Christians as "doleful." His criticism is probably due to the fact that during the nineteenth century (as in our own times) many people claimed to be Christians. However, many of those people did not practice a religion rooted in a love for God and a love for other people but rather a religion of tradition and ritual. As 2 Timothy 3: states, they gave an appearance of godliness, but they denied—through word and deed—the God who makes men godly.

Read Romans 2:17-24 aloud with your student(s). Guide him in a discussion about how strict attention to tradition rather than God's Word can cause people like Carlyle to curse the name of our Lord unnecessarily. Help him to understand the personal and social significance of Jesus's words concerning

legalism found in Matthew 23:23-28. Religious hypocrisy whether it is practiced in the first, nineteenth, or twenty-first century always causes people to curse God. Christians are called to be holy for God's sake. As His chosen people, we are to live in accordance to His Word. We are not to bind other people's consciences or our own with religious traditions or rituals not found in the Word of God. God commands us to look to His perfect Law in order to know what is required of us (cf. 2 Timothy 3:16). When we expect people to live up to laws or rules not found in God's Word we become as the Pharisees, which Jesus called "blind guides, who... outwardly appear righteous to men, but inside...are full of hypocrisy and lawlessness."

**SELF TEST 1**

| | |
|---|---|
| 1.01 | T |
| 1.02 | F |
| 1.03 | T |
| 1.04 | F |
| 1.05 | T |
| 1.06 | F |
| 1.07 | F |
| 1.08 | F |
| 1.09 | T |
| 1.010 | T |
| 1.011 | T |
| 1.012 | F |
| 1.013 | F |

| | |
|---|---|
| 1.014 | pessimistic |
| 1.015 | *Jude the Obscure*, novelist |
| 1.016 | verse forms, common people |
| 1.017 | First World War, German |
| 1.018 | orthodox Christianity |
| 1.019 | appreciated |

| | |
|---|---|
| 1.020 | a |
| 1.021 | b |
| 1.022 | c |
| 1.023 | a |
| 1.024 | a |
| 1.025 | d |
| 1.026 | b |
| 1.027 | a |
| 1.028 | b |
| 1.029 | b |
| 1.030 | d |
| 1.031 | a |

**For Thought and Discussion:**

G. K. Chesterton believed that the modern view of religion was perpetuated by "illiberal thinkers" rather than so called "liberal thinkers." He calls them "illiberal" because they don't actually think freely. They hold to a strict materialistic view of the world, which does not allow for the supernatural. Liberal thinkers or theologians in effect attempt to bind the Creator Himself, limiting Him to the laws of His own creation.

The desire of "liberal thinkers" to equate one religion with another is opposite to fact. The various religions of the world do indeed use similar methods of worship and devotion, but do not agree in the means of salvation. Chesterton pointed out in particular the differences between Buddhism and Christianity. Both acknowledge the problem of sin, however, the two systems of thought deal with it differently.

Guide your student in a discussion of Chesterton's insistence that a belief in the existence of the Triune God is western civilization's only hope for "humanity and liberty and love." Help him to understand that a belief in the transcendence of God encourages us to reform ourselves and the world around us. Chesterton states his point clearly by saying:

> "We find that in so far as we value democracy and the self-renewing energies of the west, we are much more likely to find them in the old theology than the new. If we want reform, we must adhere to orthodoxy: especially in this matter…, the matter of insisting on the immanent or the transcendent deity. By insisting specially on the immanence of God we get introspection, self-isolation, quietism, social indifference—Tibet. By insisting specially on the transcendence of God we get wonder, curiosity, moral and political adventure, righteous indignation—Christendom. Insisting that God is inside man, man is always inside himself. By insisting that God transcends man, man has transcended himself."

In light of the modern tendencies to embrace all religions in the hopes to bring about greater peace and social reform, Chesterton states, that orthodox Christianity "is the natural fountain of revolution and reform." The existence of "humanity and liberty and love" in a society is only possible when free thought within the bounds of orthodoxy is fostered

## SELF TEST 2

2.01 Irish, William Blake, Edmund Spenser
2.02 National
2.03 realistic
2.04 mystical
2.05 Ezra Pound
2.06 "stream of consciousness"
2.07 T. S. Eliot
2.08 "redeem the time"
2.09 George Bernard Shaw
2.010 socialism
2.011 army
2.012 Neville Chamberlain
2.013 courageous
2.014 grand
2.015 First World War, German
2.016 appreciated

2.017 a
2.018 c
2.019 a
2.020 c
2.021 d
2.022 b
2.023 a
2.024 a
2.025 d
2.026 a
2.027 a
2.028 c
2.029 a
2.030 a
2.031 d
2.032 a

2.033 T
2.034 T
2.035 F
2.036 T
2.037 T
2.038 F
2.039 F
2.040 T

## For Thought and Discussion:

Before his conversion to Christianity, T. S. Eliot was the most read expounder of modernism. His poems captured the hopelessness and sterility of society. In *The Love Song of J. Alfred Prufrock*, Eliot presents the modern view of love as empty and meaningless.

Guide your student in a discussion of *why* the view of love as presented in *The Love Song of J. Alfred Prufrock* is typical of modern relationships. Help your student to understand that the "absence of love" is symptomatic of "the absence of God" in society. People do not know what love is because they do not know who God is. To emphasis this point, remind your student of the works of various modern writers that underscore 1 John 4:7-19, which lead to the conclusion that God is the source of love, and without Him love is impossible. Some examples include, Thomas Hardy's poem "Neutral Tones," which implies that the "disappearance of God" from society has rendered all things lifeless, devoid of passion and meaning; or, G. K. Chesterton's statement that the insistence on the transcendent God begets moral energy and passion. "By insisting that God transcends man, man has transcended himself."

## SELF TEST 3

| | |
|---|---|
| 3.01 | progressive |
| 3.02 | Virginia Woolf |
| 3.03 | stream of consciousness |
| 3.04 | C. S. Lewis |
| 3.05 | Oxford |
| 3.06 | Christian |
| 3.07 | Irish |
| 3.08 | socialism |
| 3.09 | "Adam's Curse" |
| 3.010 | "Sailing to Byzantium" |
| 3.011 | *The Love Song of J. Alfred Prufrock* |
| 3.012 | victory |
| | |
| 3.013 | T |
| 3.014 | T |
| 3.015 | T |
| 3.016 | F |
| 3.017 | T |
| 3.018 | T |
| 3.019 | T |
| 3.020 | F |
| 3.021 | F |
| 3.022 | T |
| 3.023 | T |
| 3.024 | T |
| 3.025 | F |
| 3.026 | F |
| | |
| 3.027 | a |
| 3.028 | a |
| 3.029 | d |
| 3.030 | c |
| 3.031 | c |
| 3.032 | c |
| 3.033 | a |
| 3.034 | b |
| 3.035 | d |
| 3.036 | a |
| 3.037 | b |
| 3.038 | b |
| 3.039 | a |
| 3.040 | d |
| | |
| 3.041 | Roman Catholic |
| 3.042 | *Dubliners* |
| 3.043 | *Ulysses* |
| 3.044 | Darwinism |
| 3.045 | *Brave New World* |
| 3.046 | mysticism |
| 3.047 | G. K. Chesterton |
| 3.048 | grand |

### For Thought and Discussion:

C. S. Lewis's book The Screwtape Letters attempts to rip back the cover on the material world in order to reveal, as Lewis said, that "there is no neutral ground in the universe: every square inch, every split second, is claimed by God and counter claimed by Satan." The book is organized into a series of letters between a senior demon, Screwtape, and a junior tempter, Wormwood.

Guide your student in a discussion of the implications of Screwtape's advice to Wormwood: "The safest road to Hell is the gradual one—the gentle slope, soft underfoot, without sudden turnings, without milestones, without signposts." In light of James 1:14-15, help him to understand why Screwtape encourages the use of "small" sins over "big" sins. Though considered a "small" sin because it is not externally obvious, lust if allowed to fester in the heart will eventually "give birth to sin" and eventually grown to damning proportions. With this in mind, explain to your student why it is important to examine ourselves daily for "small" sins. Consider the implications of 2 John 2:15-17 in your answer: "If anyone loves the world, the love of the Father is not in him. For all that is in the world—the lust of the flesh, the lust of the eyes, the pride of life—is not of the Father but is of the world. And the world is passing away, and the lust of it; but he who does the will of God abides forever."

1. Old English
2. John Wycliffe
3. human
4. Italian
5. unfinished
6. plays
7. England
8. middle
9. morality
10. Mystery
11. Moralities
12. Roman Catholic
13. kenning

14. F
15. T
16. T
17. F
18. T
19. F
20. F
21. F
22. F
23. T
24. F
25. T
26. F
27. T
28. F
29. T
30. T
31. T
32. T
33. T
34. T
35. T
36. T
37. F

38. Rome
39. Anglo-Saxons
40. oral-formulaic
41. Norman
42. romance
43. heroic
44. church
45. neighbor
46. Yorkist
47. *Le Morte d' Arthur*
48. King Arthur
49. Christian
50. *Beowulf*
51. French
52. Scotland

**Thinking and Writing:**

Whichever topic is chosen, look for important facts and points that were discussed with the student during the corresponding "For Thought and Discussion" exercise. The paper should communicate the subject matter in a clear, organized manner. Correct grammar and punctuation should be used.

1. Protestant Reformers
2. Renaissance
3. literature
4. courtier
5. sonnet sequence
6. comedy
7. sonnet
8. William Tyndale
9. Queen Mary
10. wicked
11. Sir Walter Raleigh
12. oval
13. Stratford-on-Avon
14. fall
15. First Folio
16. Reformation
17. Geneva
18. King James Version

19. T
20. F
21. T
22. F
23. F
24. F
25. F
26. F
27. F
28. F
29. T
30. T
31. T
32. F
33. T
34. F
35. F
36. F

37. *Acts and Monuments*
38. *Utopia*
39. Scripture, learning
40. England
41. conceit
42. archaic, chivalry
43. The Countess of Pembroke
44. Sir Philip Sidney
45. ever-fixed
46. rare
47. Geneva
48. English
49. Henry Howard
50. Italian

**Thinking and Writing:**

Whichever topic is chosen, look for important facts and points that were discussed with the student during the corresponding "For Thought and Discussion" exercise. The paper should communicate the subject matter in a clear, organized manner. Correct grammar and punctuation should be used.

1. T
2. F
3. T
4. F
5. F
6. T
7. F
8. T
9. F
10. F
11. F
12. F
13. T
14. T
15. F
16. T

17. John Milton
18. John Dryden
19. Enlightenment
20. Jonathan Swift
21. Isaac Watts
22. Neoclassical
23. George Herbert
24. *Paradise Lost*
25. Cavalier
26. *An Essay on Man*
27. physical
28. Oliver Cromwell
29. John Donne's
30. allegories
31. parables
32. poets
33. Alexander Pope

34. Christian first comes under conviction for his sin when he is reading his book.

35. Christian's burden falls from his back when He comes to the foot of the Cross.

36. King David was the chosen ruler of Israel.

37. It assumes that people are essentially good.

38. The limitation of man's knowledge is nature.

39. The appeal and greatness of Shakespeare's work transcends the boundaries of time and culture.

40. b
41. c
42. d
43. d
44. a

**Thinking and Writing:**
Whichever topic is chosen, look for important facts and points that were discussed with the student during the corresponding "For Thought and Discussion" exercise. The paper should communicate the subject matter in a clear, organized manner. Correct grammar and punctuation should be used.

1. T
2. T
3. F
4. F
5. F
6. F
7. F
8. F
9. T
10. T
11. T
12. F
13. T
14. T
15. T
16. F
17. F

18. *Sartor Resartus*
19. strong leaders
20. *Scenes from Clerical Life*
21. Evolution
22. factory
23. *The Pickwick Papers*
24. public readings
25. *In Memoriam*, elegy
26. Alfred Lord Tennyson
27. Lewis Carroll
28. Sir Walter Scott

29. the poet-prophet or Bard

30. "The spontaneous overflow of powerful feelings."

31. The Normans and the Saxons.

32. the duke

33. to share accounts of their journeys and adventures with the members of the Pickwick Club

34. d
35. a
36. c
37. b
38. d
39. c
40. c
41. a
42. a

43. historical
44. transcendental
45. Byron's
46. *Biographia Literaria*
47. Keats
48. Shelley
49. Enlightenment
50. *The Rime of the Ancient Mariner*
51. Browning
52. *The Ring and the Book*
53. *The Importance of Being Earnest*

**Thinking and Writing:**

Whichever topic is chosen, look for important facts and points that were discussed with the student during the corresponding "For Thought and Discussion" exercise. The paper should communicate the subject matter in a clear, organized manner. Correct grammar and punctuation should be used.

1.  Virginia Woolf
2.  stream of consciousness
3.  G. K. Chesterton and C. S. Lewis
4.  Lewis
5.  Irish
6.  socialism
7.  "Adam's Curse"
8.  "Sailing to Byzantium"
9.  *The Love Song of J. Alfred Prufrock*
10. victory

11. F
12. F
13. F
14. T
15. F
16. T
17. F
18. F
19. T
20. T
21. F
22. T
23. T

24. a
25. d
26. b
27. a
28. b
29. d
30. b
31. a
32. c
33. c

34. James Joyce
35. *Dubliners*
36. Aldous Huxley
37. *Brave New World*
38. G. K. Chesterton
39. Winston Churchill
40. Thomas Hardy

## Thinking and Writing:

Whichever topic is chosen, look for important facts and points that were discussed with the student during the corresponding "For Thought and Discussion" exercise. The paper should communicate the subject matter in a clear, organized manner. Correct grammar and punctuation should be used.

| | | | |
|---|---|---|---|
| 1. | Old English | 37. | Rome |
| 2. | John Wycliffe | 38. | Anglo-Saxons |
| 3. | human | 39. | Norman |
| 4. | Italian | 40. | Middle |
| 5. | unfinished | 41. | heroic |
| 6. | plays | 42. | church |
| 7. | England | 43. | neighbor |
| 8. | middle | 44. | Yorkist |
| 9. | morality | 45. | *Le Morte d' Arthur* |
| 10. | Mystery | 46. | King Arthur |
| 11. | Moralities | 47. | worldview |
| 12. | Roman Catholic | *48.* | *Beowulf* |
| | | 49. | French |
| 13. | T | 50. | Scotland |
| 14. | F | | |
| 15. | F | | |
| 16. | T | | |
| 17. | T | | |
| 18. | T | | |
| 19. | T | | |
| 20. | T | | |
| 21. | T | | |
| 22. | F | | |
| 23. | T | | |
| 24. | F | | |
| 25. | T | | |
| 26. | F | | |
| 27. | T | | |
| 28. | F | | |
| 29. | F | | |
| 30. | F | | |
| 31. | F | | |
| 32. | F | | |
| 33. | T | | |
| 34. | F | | |
| 35. | F | | |
| 36. | T | | |

| | | | | |
|---|---|---|---|---|
| 1. | Scripture | 37. | historical |
| 2. | Renaissance | 38. | *Utopia* |
| 3. | Elizabethan | 39. | Scripture, learning |
| 4. | courtier | 40. | England |
| 5. | sonnet sequence | 41. | conceit |
| 6. | comedy, amuse | 42. | archaic, chivalry |
| 7. | sonnet | 43. | divine |
| 8. | William Tyndale | 44. | Sir Philip Sidney |
| 9. | Mary, Protestants | 45. | ever-fixed |
| 10. | wicked | 46. | rare |
| 11. | poet | 47. | Geneva Bible |
| 12. | oval | 48. | English |
| 13. | Stratford-on-Avon | 49. | three |
| 14. | fall | 50. | fourteen, octave |
| 15. | First Folio, 1623 | | |
| 16. | Reformation | | |
| 17. | Geneva Bible | | |
| 18. | King James Version, people | | |
| 19. | F | | |
| 20. | T | | |
| 21. | F | | |
| 22. | T | | |
| 23. | T | | |
| 24. | T | | |
| 25. | T | | |
| 26. | T | | |
| 27. | T | | |
| 28. | T | | |
| 29. | F | | |
| 30. | F | | |
| 31. | F | | |
| 32. | T | | |
| 33. | F | | |
| 34. | T | | |
| 35. | T | | |
| 36. | T | | |

| | | | | |
|---|---|---|---|---|
| 1. | F | | 32. | a |
| 2. | T | | 33. | b |
| 3. | F | | 34. | d |
| 4. | T | | 35. | b |
| 5. | T | | 36. | c |
| 6. | F | | 37. | a |
| 7. | T | | 38. | b |
| 8. | F | | 39. | c |
| 9. | T | | 40. | b |
| 10. | T | | 41. | b |
| 11. | T | | 42. | a |
| 12. | T | | 43. | c |
| 13. | F | | 44. | b |
| 14. | F | | 45. | c |

15. Parliamentary supporter
16. Neoclassical
17. Enlightenment
18. Tory
19. hymns, hymnody
20. Neoclassical
21. poetry
22. *Paradise Lost*
23. Cavalier
24. physical
25. Oliver Cromwell
26. metaphysical
27. allegories
28. preaching
29. Bible
30. Greek, Roman
31. man

1. F
2. F
3. T
4. T
5. T
6. T
7. T
8. T
9. T
10. F
11. F
12. T
13. F
14. F
15. F
16. T
17. T

18. *Sartor Resartus*
19. strong leaders
20. *Scenes from Clerical Life*
21. Evolution
22. factory, unpaid debts
23. *The Pickwick Papers*
24. public readings of his works
25. *In Memoriam,* elegy
26. Tennyson
27. the three Liddell daughters
28. legal official

29. b
30. c
31. a
32. b
33. c
34. a
35. a
36. b
37. a
38. b
39. d
40. c
41. c
42. d

43. historical
44. transcendental
45. relativity
46. *Biographia Literaria*
47. art
48. imagination
49. Enlightenment
50. *The Rime of the Ancient Mariner*
51. Elizabeth Barrett
52. *The Ring and the Book*
53. *The Importance of Being Earnest*

1. Virginia Woolf
2. stream of consciousness
3. C. S. Lewis
4. Christianity
5. Irish
6. socialism
7. "Adam's Curse"
8. "Sailing to Byzantium"
9. *The Love Song of J. Alfred Prufrock*
10. victory

11. T
12. T
13. T
14. F
15. T
16. F
17. T
18. T
19. F
20. F
21. F
22. T
23. F
24. F

25. d
26. c
27. c
28. a
29. b
30. a
31. b
32. d
33 a
34. c

35. Roman Catholic
36. *Dubliners*
37. Darwinism
38. *Brave New World*
39. G. K. Chesterton
40. grand
41. verse forms, common people

# British Litera
# Teacher's Guide

## CONTENTS

**Author:**      **Krista L. White, B.S.**

Editor:      Alan Christopherson, M.S.

Alpha Omega Publications®

804 N. 2nd Ave. E., Rock Rapids, IA 51246-1759